THE DOVE C

Whistling Wings

H. ELLIOTT McCLURE

THE BOXWOOD PRESS

Distributed by:

THE BOXWOOD PRESS
183 Ocean View Boulevard
Pacific Grove, CA 93950

Phone: (408) 375-9110
Fax: (408) 375-0430

ISBN: 0-940168-19-7

Drawings by Karen Morgan

Library of Congress Cataloging-in-Publication Data:
McClure, Elliott.
   Whistling wings / H. Elliott McClure.
      p.   cm.
   Includes bibliographical references.
   ISBN 0-940168-19-7
   1. Mourning dove.   I. Title.
QL696.C63M37   1991
598'.65–dc20   91-16128
                                                CIP

Printed in U.S.A.

Foreword

$\mathcal{M}$ANY years ago a friend gave me a ring-necked turtle dove chick. He told me that it had been rejected by its parents, which he kept caged. Would I like to raise it?

At the time I was surprised to hear that parent birds would reject their young. Now, however, after reading Elliott McClure's book, I can understand why. Each sex has its role to play in rearing chicks. Mother doves stay with their young during the night and are relieved after twelve hours by their mates, who work the day shift. By contrast, caged parents never get any time off from their young or from each other, for that matter. Who wouldn't get testy?

I wish I had read Elliott McClure's description of the life of mourning doves before I took in that foundling chick. I would have been a better foster mother. Although mine was not a mourning dove, but a turtle dove, the two species are closely related and behave in much the same manner. Armed with the detailed knowledge that this wonderful book contains, I would have been able to offer my bird a better life.

Instead I bumbled along. For twelve years my bird filled my rooms with beautiful cooing sounds, meant to attract a mate. Once she even built a nest of shredded paper and laid two eggs in it. Of course, they were not fertile eggs. She never met a male bird. I often let her fly about the house and she loved to land on my head. She also liked to warm herself under a lightbulb. She should have been alighting on leafy branches and taking sunbaths. After reading about the rich life that wild doves enjoy, these memories pain me more. For, despite the many disasters that befall the wild birds in this book, their lives are meaningful. Each bird is committed to the preservation of its life and kind. It applies all of its energy and skill toward that end. And each morning when it wakes to see another day it pours its throat in celebration of being alive.

Yet as well-equipped as this species is to meet natural calamities, the mourning dove is no match for humans. Our ballooning population is robbing these birds of their homes and their food sources. Many people take pleasure in shooting enormous numbers of doves as they make their annual journey south. Elliott McClure's book ought to be required reading for all who engage in such "sport." For his account of dove life leaves one with a profound sense of the value of each and every bird. It is an important message.

- Hope Ryden

Hope Ryden is author of *God's Dog* and other wildlife stories.

Preface

$\mathcal{T}$HESE are stories about Mourning Doves and how they survive in the world of humans. I have tried to select some of the many things that enter into the life of a dove, its problems, and solutions. These examples are all taken from 50 years of observations of doves in North America and Asia and from studies of more than 5,000 Mourning Dove nestings. I have foreshortened the time element in some instances and have assumed the birds' abilities to communicate. In the past 50 years a vast amount of research has been conducted, both observational and experimental in effort to learn if and how animals communicate. Studies with the higher primates and dolphins have attempted communication between humans and animals, with limited success. It is obvious that birds, including doves, watch and listen to other species and "know" their signals, responding to them in case of danger or other situations.

It is still a mystery how birds become aware of food supplies beyond the horizon. That they watch the actions of others of their own or different species does not fully explain this. Mourning Doves communicate with a variety of sounds and body signals, but it is doubtful if they can transmit more complex thoughts or ideas. They have accurate memories of breeding and wintering territories as well as the routes between them. We do not know if this information is transmitted between them. All through the story I have let Zee and others communicate by an exchange of ideas, that is,"talk." This anthropomorphic (human-like) approach is subject to criticism, but by using this method I have avoided belaboring the incidents related with long explanations and descriptions.

Zee and Naida and their "friends" are lovely, blue-gray Mourning Doves with pointed white-tipped tails and iridiscent feathers on the neck and breast. As adults they have sky-blue skin around the eyes, salmon red mouths and coral-red feet, while on the folded wings darker brown spots easily distinguish them from other doves of similar size.

Mourning Doves are of ancient origin, probably from lower Miocene dove-like ancestors of some 30 million years ago. Mourning Doves are distributed throughout North America from Central America into the southern Canadian provinces. They are not large birds, weighing about a quarter of a pound (120 grams); those east of the Rocky Mountains are somewhat heavier and paler than their smaller and darker cousins of the Pacific Coast.

Before the colonization of America by Europeans, Mourning Doves were forest-edge birds, being most abundant in the midwest where the great forests met the prairie. As the forests were cut back and reduced to remnants, the doves increased and became town and farmyard birds.

H. Elliott McClure

Camarillo, California
Spring 1991

Contents

CHAPTER ONE

Zee and Naida

*A*S the stars faded before the first true light of a soft June dawn, Zee, high in an elm tree, awoke from one of his short "cat-naps," swallowed, yawned, extended his neck and stretched lazily. He raised his wings over his back, exposing the beautiful blue-gray of his sides. Then he stretched his right leg and wing to the rear as far as he could. After this he balanced himself on the right leg and extended his left leg and wing. Finally he again raised his wings over his back. It was a new day, and clouds on the southwestern horizon predicted a squall. Ignoring the weather, Zee turned to preening. A good, dog-like shake scattered loose feather scales, and then, from neck to tail each feather was combed through the bill and prop-

1

erly placed. A couple of loose feathers he pulled out and dropped, watching them zigzag to the ground.

Other males in nearby trees were accomplishing their toilets and occasionally one or another cooed. As the sky brightened and sunlight spun the morning mists to golden foam, cooing increased to a crescendo. Zee joined the chorus from the tip of the highest dead branch of his tree. His full-throated, five-noted coo could be distinguished from that of other singers. It was a fine, quiet morning. Zee was in splendid health, so he cooed steadily for ten or fifteen minutes, at the rate of two calls a minute, warning other males that this was his territory. He expressed his joy, and told the world in general that here was a Mourning Dove.

Abruptly he ceased cooing and sailed down to the weedy edge of a garden not two hundred meters from his sleeping place. This was his particular feeding ground, included in his territory, and rarely, if ever, transgressed by other doves. Weeds abounded and he fell to picking up seeds of sorrel, hemp, ragweed, pigweed, and yellow foxtail. Stopping but for seconds to look about, he consumed fifty seeds a minute and walked about eating for fifteen minutes. From the corner of his eye he caught sight of a black cat creeping cautiously through the grass toward him. Continuing to feed unconcernedly, Zee walked from the grass into the open garden. There he could better watch the cat. With only the tip of his tail twitching, the cat stalked closer. Zee walked away a few steps and picked up more seeds. The cat quivered forward and Zee fed along, keeping the same distance between them. Suspense began to tell on the cat. It hurried a few paces and the dove scampered along, snatching at a seed as he went by. The cat stopped and the dove stopped, but the bird dropped his wings to loosen them for flight. With an irritated swish of its tail, the cat charged, and Zee rose on whistling wings to the nearest apple tree.

Interrupting his breakfast irritated Zee and for several minutes he sat on this limb watching the cat, berating it with rapid, almost inaudible guttural notes deep in his throat. The cat soon disappeared around a house. Zee promptly forgot it and returned to preening. As his dry breakfast had made him thirsty, Zee flew with strong, swift wingbeats to his usual drinking place, the bank of a small stream bordered by trees, nearly a kilometer away. After assuring himself that no enemies were near, he dropped to the bank and walked to the water's edge. Immersing his bill and mouth clear to his face, Zee sucked up a great gulp of water, looked about, then drank again. There was still no danger evident, allowing him to stroll along the streamside picking up a few tiny snail shells. He flew to the trees and finally, as rapidly as he had come, returned to his territory.

From a nearby red pine came a single high shrill coo. It was past seven o'clock and Naida, Zee's mate, was tired of her long night's vigil on the nest. She was hungry and the two six-day-old young beneath her were squirming in hope of being fed. Zee flew to the limb, a fork of which supported their nest about five meters from the ground, walked out on it to Naida's side and began clucking to her. They conversed in rapid, low notes, then Naida stepped from the nest. She fluttered invitingly and quivered her wings while Zee billed with her and preened the feathers of her neck and shoulders. The two youngsters, sitting side by side, but facing opposite directions, watched their parents in hungry anticipation. Zee stepped to the edge of the nest and emitted a soft call, while Naida flew away to her feeding ground. Instantly the nest was seething with scrambling babies. Crying a shrill chick-like peep, stretching their necks and flapping their half-clad wings, they clamored to be fed. The older nestling thrust its bill into Zee's mouth. Zee fed it by pumping seeds, water, and a clear secretion from his crop walls, known as "pigeon milk," into its throat. The nestling flapped and strained to be fed further, but Zee turned his attention to the younger one. Both became very excited and finally he was feeding them, each with its bill at the sides of his mouth. Satisfied, they settled back in the hollow of the nest and Zee stepped between them, fluffing his breast and belly feathers so that the little birds were completely covered except for two heads projecting from under his breast. The youngsters rested their heads upon their own distended crops, which protruded shelf-like beneath their chins; this load of food and water nearly equal to half of their weights.

Naida's feeding ground was closer to the nest tree and in the opposite direction from that of Zee's. She fed, drank from a nearby bird bath, and returned to roost upon a telephone wire near the nest. About this small midwestern town in Iowa, other doves rested on wires or limbs, inadvertently advertising the proximity of their nests. Here Naida preened, going through all of the motions her mate had performed earlier in the day.

By now it was midmorning and the storm, heralded at dawn by thunderheads in the west, was moving in. Gusts of a strong southwest wind swayed the tree and strained the limb supporting Zee and his brood. The young birds huddled close together and clung to the nest with their strong feet. Zee squatted lower over them and he, too, gripped the nest materials. As it was early summer, such sudden thundershowers were not unusual and this location had weathered several. He and Naida could not know that the limb was decayed at its base. A sudden gust of wind snapped the limb and dropped it, spilling the nest's occupants. Zee took flight and alighted on a nearby limb while the two young fluttered their wings in a vain effort to fly, but pin feathers gave them no support. One fell directly to the hard ground, rupturing its crop, and with a few gasps it died. The other struck a twig and fell spinning, but unhurt.

Rain fell heavily for an hour, during which Zee and Naida sat on a limb with heads raised, allowing the water to run off their faces to their backs and throats. The storm ceased as abruptly as it had begun and both birds shook water from their feathers, spread their wings in the sun, and flew about for a few moments. Then they returned to the site of their nest, uttering low cooing notes as they surveyed the havoc wrought by the storm. On the ground was their family, one dead and the other apparently drowned. As they watched, a man came by and picked up the tiny birds. Cupped in the warmth of his hands, the half-drowned youngster showed signs of life as he carried it away.

The parents flew about aimlessly for a few minutes and then quieted down to roost in an elm until nearly four o'clock. By this time, the sting of their loss had eased and they turned to their evening meal. Naida accompanied Zee to feed at his grounds, and they drank their fill from puddles in the garden. In walking among the grass, Naida found many shells of tiny land snails and ate them, for soon she would be laying again and she needed lime for her egg shells. After their supper, Zee flew to his cooing perch and joined other males in their evening song. Naida apparently paid no attention but sat quietly and preened. With the setting sun, Zee gave a few final calls and then dropped to the side of his mate.

The night was quiet and they roosted together undisturbed. With the light of another day, Zee felt the breath of romance; the summer was still young and many babies could yet be raised. He mounted to his cooing site and voiced his emotions loudly. Having uttered several calls, he leaped into the air and with great whistling strokes flew in a straight steep climb for a hundred meters. At the peak of this climb, he banked to the left and with wings outstretched soared gracefully back to his perch. He cooed and repeated this performance, time and again indulging in these graceful flights. But Naida kept feeding in the garden. At the end of one of these prowess demonstrations, he swooped down to alight beside her. She fluttered her wings in recognition for she had been watching him all of the time.

As he picked up a few seeds she sidled up to him, shaking her wings and begging. He also quivered his wings and strutted around her. Every few steps he stopped and rubbed his beak in the feathers of his flanks behind his wings. Closing her eyes, Naida stepped up to him, bobbing her head in a gesture to preen the feathers of his neck. Then she rubbed her bill in the feathers of her flanks. He, with his eyes shut, preened her neck and back. As their ardor intensified, they centered their preening more and more about the head and mouth. A noise disturbed them and they ceased their courting to look about. Satisfied that no danger lurked near, the courting was resumed. This time she lowered her head and he placed his bill over hers and fed her. As she was fed, she squatted, dropped her wings and he mounted her back. They copulated. He hopped from her back and strutted a few steps, emitting a shrill, hoarse, undove-like "kah." She, too, made this sound and they fell to conversing rapidly in low tones. They preened for a moment and then continued with their breakfasts.

Three times they mated this day and three times the next. On the eighth day after their loss of home and young, Naida informed Zee that nest building time had arrived. After breakfast he went in search of another suitable nesting place within his territory. He flew from tree to tree examining limbs and crotches, but he seemed to have tried them all before. Their first nest had been in a grape vine, but a cold wind had turned it over when the eggs were ten days old. Finally, he found a hollow formed by the joining of two branches of a large elm. He stepped into it, squatting down as if incubating. The place seemed all right if he let his long tail stick out of the openings, but it was a little uncomfortable in other positions.

In a large, dying Silver Maple Zee located another hollow formed by two upright branches. This site was more comfortable, so he cooed to Naida to come examine it. After a few calls from him, she flew to his side while he proudly exhibited the site of his selection. Naida tried the hollow, turning about fussily and then with what appeared to be disgust stepped from it. He courted her for a few minutes and they flew away. He had better hurry and find a good place, for the first egg was almost mature.

More searching, then he saw a site that was just right. A pair of robins were industriously completing a nest on the limb of an apple tree. While the owners were away gathering mud and grass, Zee alighted on the nest and found it to his liking. Naida responded to his call and was inspecting the nest when one of the robins returned. It was nonplussed at the change of events, dropped its load and flew away when Naida flapped at it. Several times the robins returned, finally to give up and fly away.

Zee was activated by Naida's approval of his selection. She remained on the nest while he flew to the ground and hurried about looking for nest materials. Surely the new robin nest was better than their old scant one, but even so, they must add to it. Zee picked up a twig and tried it with his beak, rapidly biting it to test its size and weight. Dissatisfied, he dropped it and ran on a few steps to try another. After three or four twigs had been tested, one proved satisfactory. He grasped it at its center and flew in a straight climbing flight to a nearby limb of the nest tree. Glancing about for enemies, he dropped to the limb where the nest was situated and walked to Naida's side. He hopped to the middle of her back and from there reached forward to place the twig in front of her. Then he jumped from her back, walked out on the limb and flew to his job of finding more material. Naida seized the twig and placed it beneath her. In a moment Zee was back with another to place before her. This, too, she pushed beneath her feet.

Zee continued to return at about one-minute intervals. When he seemed to have tested all available material in one place, he flew to another nearby, always returning to hop on Naida's back to place the piece before her. After more than an hour of this, the nest was beginning to take form and Naida was busy crossing and recrossing the twigs and grasses and patting them with her feet. The diameter of building material Zee brought was becoming smaller, and finally the cup was lined with grass. However, it was past 10 o'clock and they were both tiring of their work. Zee was startled by a dog as he flew toward the nest, and dropped the blade of grass he was carrying. He landed near the nest and Naida called to him. They flew off together. Two hours later they could be seen in the garden having a bite of lunch.

The next morning, before Zee had finished his breakfast, Naida was on the nest calling to him for more grass. He worked diligently for a few minutes, then a spot strewn with choice seeds attracted his attention. His snack was interrupted by a high shrill call from the nest, so he returned to his job. By eight o'clock he had brought enough twigs to considerably augment yesterday's work, but Naida seemed to have lost interest in the activity. She hovered low over the nest while he flew to another tree for a nap.

As the morning progressed, Naida began to look ill. She moved heavily, and a hump near the base of her tail, which had become conspicuous yesterday, seemed larger. Near noon she stood up, her body shook, her tail rotated, and she deposited a creamy white egg. Rolling it beneath her breast with her slender bill, she began incubating. Zee did not disturb her all day long, but when she left the nest for her four o'clock feeding, he accompanied her to his feeding place. She ate hurriedly and in a few moments returned to the nest. She incubated all night and until the second egg was laid the next evening.

Now a daily routine was set up. Zee incubated from eight or nine in the morning until four or five in the afternoon, Naida from four p.m. to eight a.m. During the first few days of incubation, if something startled Zee, he would fly off and remain away as long as an hour. But as the embryos developed, both birds became more attentive and it was difficult to frighten them from the he nest. Had Naida been driven from her duties at night, she would have not returned and the eggs would have chilled.

A robin's* nest is substantial, and the one appropriated by the doves weathered several storms. On the thirteenth day after the first egg was laid, a young bird hatched. Early in the morning, Naida heard the tapping of this baby as it struck against the inner shell with its egg tooth. Soon these blows resulted in a dent in the shell near the large end. The birdlet rotated a little and pecked again. After more than an hour small dents nearly encircled the egg. The work was hard and the worker rested often. Meanwhile Zee took Naida's place and hovered over the eggs. It was eight hours after the first dent appeared before the young dove exerted enough pressure against the shell to pop off the lid it had created. It lay exhausted in the opened shell, wet, and sparsely covered with yellow

---

* All through these stories "robin" refers to the American Robin, *Turdus migratorius*. It is a larger bird than the Robin, *Erithacus rubecula*, common throughout Europe. Both species are town and garden birds.

down. It's eyes were shut, it breathed rapidly, and it was unable to raise its head. On the tip of its slender black bill was a large, white, sharply-pointed tooth, the egg tooth, a special tool for escaping the egg. Zee reached under his breast and helped the young bird work free of its shell and kept the youngster warm while it dried.

Lewis, Iowa. Such small midwestern towns are favored homes of Mourning Doves.

Shortly after the hatchling was free, Zee picked up the shell and, carrying it round end forward, flew from the nest. At a distance of several meters, he dropped it and returned to the nest. In the meantime, Naida had returned and was already brooding. She stepped off after a few minutes and her mate took over his duties. He picked up the remaining egg-cap, dropped it over the side, and turned to feeding the young bird its first meal. The birdlet was upright beneath him, but its head lay to one side. Zee stimulated it to shakily raise its head by touching its bill, which he then took in his mouth. Lowering his head, he gently worked his crop so that pigeon milk spilled slowly into the young one's throat. After a few swallows Zee released the small bird's bill. A few hours later the youngster was fed again, and so on through the day. Naida took over its care in the afternoon, and by nightfall its crop was filled. Sometime during the night the infant demanded more.

CHAPTER TWO
Ha-Wo

ABOUT the same time the next morning the second bird hatched and the procedure was repeated. Had either baby hatched while Naida was present, the shells would have remained until Zee came to remove them, or she would have called to him for this chore. By now, the first baby, Ha-wo (the Shoshoni Indian word for dove) could hold up its head and it had a 24-hour start on the second, Wa-u-ia-uk (Selish for dove), but they were both very healthy and weighed six grams each (about one-fifth of an ounce). Each day they gained as much as they weighed at hatching, or from five to six grams a day. Ha-wo weighed twelve grams when Wa-u-ia-uk emerged and was six or more grams ahead of him all during their nestling life.

For the first six days, Zee and Naida did not greatly alter their habits. They fed the youngsters morning, noon, and evening and more often if they cried for it. Ha-wo, being older and stronger, always demanded the first feeding, but neither parent favored him and they always saw that Wa-u-ia-uk received his share. Zee continued to brood from eight a.m. to four p.m. and Naida from four p.m. to eight a.m.

Development of the two youngsters was rapid. On the first day, they were too weak to hold up their heads, their skins were gray, the head and face were nearly black, their eyes were closed and they were sparsely covered with a dark cream down. The second day they could hold up their heads and the primary feathers at the very tips of their wings began to grow. From now on, these feathers grew a centimeter in length each day (two-fifths of an inch), until each wing extended more than 13 centimeters (over five inches) when they left the nest on the 13th day.

On the third day, the feathers of their tails began to grow and their eyes to open at the inner corners. At hatching they could make a faint peeping noise, and by the time they were four days old, they could cry shrilly, especially when hungry. During their fourth day, their eyes opened and they began to take an interest in their surroundings. The pinfeathers of their wings, body, head, and tail were growing and replacing down. By now, too, the egg-tooth was disappearing. It may have been resorbed by the bird or was dissolved a little at each feeding.

When five days old, more of their feathers had sprouted over the breast, flanks, back, wings, tail, and head. Their skin, except for that of the face, had faded to a pale gray. By the sixth day, the egg-tooth was completely dissolved and both youngsters were taking a lively interest in their surroundings. Their wings were well-clad, the feathers opening at the tips, which gave them a less than animated pincushion appearance. Personalities were developing as well. Ha-wo was alert and had a bright, excited look about him, while Wa-u-ia-uk looked on sleepily and rarely became perturbed, even at mealtime.

When Ha-wo was six days old, this day was one of many events. Zee did not come directly to the nest and feed the nestlings, as was his habit. Instead, he came earlier and cooed to Naida, coaxing her away. She was willing to leave, for by now both youngsters were warmly "clothed" and could be left alone for a short time. The pair flew to the treetops where he preened her, and showed his ardor by making a few acrobatic flights. This lovemaking culminated with mating and then they flew to a new place that Zee had found where seeds and snails were plentiful. It was nearly ten o'clock before he returned to the nest to find both youngsters famished and a little cold. After their long wait they received an extra feeding. During the first two days of life the nestlings were fed pigeon milk and little else. Now they were given a mixture of pigeon milk and whatever seeds their parents had eaten. With the seeds were more tiny snail shells, for growing birds must have calcium and salts for the development of their bones.

Towards the middle of the afternoon there was a great commotion in the apple tree. A man was climbing up toward them. Zee had seen him approach and had crouched low on the nest to be as inconspicuous as possible. As the man climbed closer, Zee suddenly burst from the nest and dropped to the ground. He crawled along with his wings fluttering and dragging as if broken. The man, familiar with this broken-wing ruse, did not follow, but Zee continued to drag his wings and stagger along for several meters. Uttering low warning notes, he ran about excitedly and finally flew to a nearby limb to watch.

Ha-wo was an interested spectator to all of this activity and leaned over to watch. The man seemed bent on climbing right to the nest. As he reached out to take ahold of him, Ha-wo could stand the suspense no longer.

He scrambled across the nest over the opposite side. Fortunately the nest was only three meters above the grass-cushioned ground and he alighted unhurt, to run for a few steps and hide among the plants. This availed him naught, for the man climbed down, picked him up, and placed a shining piece of metal around one of his legs. Then the man carried him back up to the nest and placed him beside Wa-u-ia-uk, who had submitted to being banded without a struggle. Ha-wo, tired and frightened by his experience, clung close to Wa-u-ia-uk.

Young dove receives a ring from the man who bands doves.

From a nearby tree, another interested spectator had been watching quietly and no sooner had the man left than this spectator, a marauding blue jay, swooped down to kill the youngsters. Here was a problem with which Zee could cope and, with a silence born of fury, he attacked the jay, knocking him bodily from the nest. Following this advantage, Zee struck the would-be assassin time and again with both wings. It was more from the suddenness of the attack than from injury that the jay quickly withdrew. Had Zee not been so prompt with his defense, both babies would have been killed and carried away.

The two were left alone more and more while their parents courted and mated, but the blue jay was never around when Zee and Naida left, and they usually remained within sight of the nest. Ha-wo and his brother did not mind being alone, for their feathers were growing and they did not get cold. Besides, they liked to stretch their wings and exercise in their small confines. They had not yet learned how to preen and both Zee and Naida spent hours each day preening them and removing loosened feather scales. By the ninth day, they had begun to help in this preening and in addition, they walked about on the nest and flapped their wings, all but falling off time and again. Even their bellies were becoming feathered, almost the last place on which feathers grow. Their skin had lost its grayness and was now pink, all but that of the face. No feathers grew about the mouth. This method of sanitation has evolved to prevent fermentation of food matted or spilled there and permits the gray skin to blend with the gray feathers of the head. It would be several days after they fledged before their faces would be fully feathered.

Now, too, the youngsters had learned about nest sanitation. Their parents did not defecate all the long hours that they were on the nest, but the youngsters, of course, deposited feces wherever they happened to be. To prevent the nest from becoming filthy, the parents swallowed the nestlings droppings or threw them out, but by the time the young were five days old they had learned to back to the edge of the nest and defecate over it.

When Ha-wo was ten days old his parents were not about when the man came by again. The little bird became excited and jumped from the nest, flying in a long slope until he landed in some weeds several meters from the apple tree. The man walked about looking for him, but he had run under heavy weeds and could not be seen. After the man had gone, Ha-wo began to regret his rash act. The surroundings were all new and strange, and, from the safety of his home, he had seen cats prowling these thickets. He felt like crying out, but was afraid to. In fact, all he dared do was remain where he was. Soon Naida returned to the nest. Zee often made her brood during the day as well as at night now. Uttering low notes of concern, she looked about for Ha-wo and, assuring herself that Wa-u-ia-uk was all right, she gave a shrill call. As he sprang up and ran into sparse grass, Naida saw him and called again. It was much farther up to the nest than it had been down, but he must try to make it. With rapid wing beats he jumped into the air and flew toward the nest, missing it by several feet, struck a limb and tumbled back to the ground. Again his mother called and again he tried. Finally, on the third trial, he managed to catch the limb and creep along it to the nest where both Naida and Wa-u-ia-uk greeted him. For once Wa-u-ia-uk had beaten him to a meal. As an incentive his mother had fed his brother openly while he fought to regain his haven. Full fed, he settled down with Wa-u-ia-uk.

The final three days before fledging, the young birds' nest life changed radically. Their parents came and went several times during each day, often brooding only an hour or so before changing places with one another. Naida still brooded at night, either beside the nest or between the youngsters, but Zee was so restless that he could not endure an all-day assignment. During the heat of the day one of the adults sometimes rested at the edge of the nest.

On the twelfth day both youngsters not only exercised but walked out and back along the supporting limb. Naida was quiet and hovered in the vicinity, for she was becoming heavy with eggs again. Each young bird was now fully clothed with buff-tipped feathers and their wings were strong enough to support them, but their tails were short and stubby, hardly suggesting the beautiful plumes that they would eventually become.

Naida left the nest at dawn of the thirteenth day and when Zee did come to bring their breakfast, he only half fed them, leaving them hungry and worried. Uttering a sharp call, he flew from the nest and Ha-wo, with his usual rashness, followed him; but Wa-u-ia-uk did not want to leave the security of his fragile home. Zee called and called, making numerous trips to the nest to coax him away. Finally, Naida entered into the discussion and both birds tried to get him to try his wings, but it was to no avail. With failing patience both parents flew to one of their feeding grounds, leaving him unfed. Ha-wo followed and watched hungrily as they picked up seeds. If he ran up to one and begged he was either ignored or rebuked with a peck, which would send him away to squat down and sulk. Soon pangs of hunger would drive him to try again. Finally, Naida relented and fed him sparingly; then she returned to the nest, leaving him under the ministration of his father.

Zee walked along and picked up a hemp seed that he tested by biting at it rapidly with the tip of his bill and striking it with his tongue. Then he dropped it. Ha-wo, watching closely, picked up the seed and swallowed it. As Zee picked up seeds of smartweed, foxtail, sorrel, and ragweed and repeated the tasting process, Ha-wo followed and ate those that his father had dropped. In the meantime, he had begun to peck at things on the ground and to try them for edibility. By the time his father had finished feeding, he had learned of several things that he could safely eat.

Having his fill, Zee led Ha-wo to the nearest water, the bird bath, since he did not feel that the youngster was capable of the long flight to the creek. After drinking Ha-wo returned to the nest. His father found a convenient roost, while Naida spent the rest of the day with her two sons.

The following morning, the fourteenth day for Ha-wo and the thirteenth for Wa-u-ia-uk, Zee came to the nest early, called to the two young and flew from the garden. They both followed. Naida went to her feeding ground and then returned to the nest. She was to lay an egg this day and the next, thereby beginning the pair's fourth nesting attempt. The training of the youngsters therefore fell on Zee's shoulders, and he spent most of the day teaching them what they could and could not eat. By evening they were self-sufficient enough to no longer need his supervision. After they had fed and watered, they returned to the nest, but Naida refused to allow them on it, wing slapping and pecking them. In distress, they were forced to sleep on a limb nearby. For almost a week, each sundown found them fore and aft together on this twig. Toward the end of the week, they struck up an acquaintance with young from other families and for two or three days roosted with their band of doves, six in all, beneath a lilac shrub.

Summer was hurrying through July, and early migration was at hand. Struck by wanderlust, the little band flew from their natal town into surrounding country, where they met other small bands in a large field of new-cut wheat. Augmenting their diet with many kinds of weed seeds, they fed here for several days and the band grew in numbers until over seventy-five young birds were present. During the last of July, the band dwindled as individual birds or siblings joined the ever-increasing flow of juvenile birds flying southward. Among these loose and often attenuated flocks was an occasional adult that had lost its mate or met with some other insurmountable breeding problem. In this flight the young birds covered but a few miles each day, often retracing routes that they had taken yesterday. They flew from tree to tree until they found fields of food where they could stop and forage. Gradually the flights focused to the south and by the end of August, Ha-wo found himself far south with birds from Minnesota, North Dakota, and Nebraska crossing the Red River into Texas.

CHAPTER THREE

Later in the Year

ZEE had paid little attention to his two offspring while they roosted near the nest, although he did occasionally allow them to follow him to his feeding ground. After they left the roost and joined the other young birds he no longer saw or came in contact with them. Naida laid her eggs, the seventh and eighth for this year, and the routine of nest life began again as it had before. The nest, having already been occupied by young, was an untidy mess of feather scales, dried feces, and other debris. Zee brought a few twigs and blades of grass, which Naida arranged so that she could roll her eggs upon a somewhat cleaner pad.

In the adjoining territory, a pair had recently finished rearing a family and had built another nest. The female had laid the first egg of this clutch and during the night a gust of wind had blown the nest from the tree leaving her with a mature egg and no place to deposit it. During the morning she had been flying urgently from tree to tree at a loss to know where to deposit her egg. She happened to alight in the apple tree and saw Zee incubating. It was day four and he was nodding in the comfort and security of his nook. The stranger quickly dropped to the nest and tried to drive him from it. Assaulted both emotionally and physically, he struck back with his wings. A wing-slapping wrestle ensued with much grunting and guttural tones, knocking Zee backward from the limb. He had to release his hold on the nest for fear of tipping it. The stranger immediately stepped into his place and laid the egg that she was holding. Zee returned, indignant at this imposition, slapped her with both wings and pecked her about the face and head. All she did was shut her eyes and pull her head down to take the beating while she laid her egg. Within a few seconds, she stepped off the nest and, with Zee slapping and following her, dropped to the ground to recuperate. Zee returned to the nest to incubate the three eggs.

Thirteen days after Naida's eggs had been laid, the first youngster hatched, and the next day the second. As these two grew, they pushed the remaining egg to one side, chilling it. They grew to fledgling age without any mishaps and left the nest when fourteen days old. It was August and their parents took a short rest. For more than a week they flew to the country, feeding in several stubble fields, picking up wheat kernels, and roosting in a nearby woods.

They were feeding upon spilled wheat when Zee noticed a dove on the ground. Flying more closely he saw that it was another male and that he was setting upon eggs. The nest, if it could be called such, was between two rows of cut wheat stems and partially shaded by a ragweed.

"How could this be?" thought Zee, "no dove would want to risk the dangers on the soil when hazards in trees are bad enough!" The stranger was surly about it, but said that his wife had dropped an egg when feeding here and had decided to remain with it. A few days later Zee learned that the young had hatched, but had been taken at night by a skunk that happened upon the family.

In another part of the field, Zee and Naida found a second couple that had a ground nest in the shelter of a small stack of hay. The male admitted that, on a trip from town, this had looked like a good place. It was early morning and his mate was still on the nest sheltering two healthy ten-day-olds who flew safely from the field with their parents before Zee and Naida returned to town.

Following their vacation, Naida was again gravid, urging that they return to town for their fifth nesting. Many doves were vacationing, allowing Zee to establish a new territory within a kilometer of the previous one and without much competition. Numerous nest losses, or loss of a mate may make a male seek a new territory at anytime.

Zee found a suitable crotch in a large elm and the two eggs were laid. This tree was across the street from a walnut which was bearing nearly ripe fruit. Not only were woodpeckers and jays attracted, but fox squirrels as well. These beautiful animals scampered all over the neighborhood, raiding bird feeders, investigating garbage cans, and exploring all of the shade trees. High in the doves' tree House Sparrows had built a bulky nest of straw and grass. One day, much scolding and disturbance attended the squirrel that found this nest and stole the eggs. Naida's eggs were half through incubation when the same or another squirrel strutted out along the limb. At first he did not see the nest, but as he drew close, Zee squatted lower and the squirrel saw this slight movement. Stopping nearby, he looked at it for a moment and Zee raised the wing opposite the invader in a feinting motion, low-ered his head, fluffed his feathers and expanded his body to its fullest extent, while he uttered a clucking sound not unlike that of an irritated hen. Unintimidated, the squir-rel pounced upon him and Zee struck with his wings as he fell from the nest, hitting the invader several times. Pitched into the air this way, Zee took flight and landed on a nearby limb from which he could watch the enemy. Holding an egg in his forepaws as if it were a nut, the squirrel bit it open and licked it clean of contents. Having finished with this egg, he dropped the shell, which floated to the ground. He then picked up the second and repeated the process.

When the bird-bander approached later in the day, he could tell by these empty shells who had been the culprit that had destroyed this latest effort by Zee and Naida. If there were no shells present, it was difficult for him deter-mine which predator had attacked. As soon as the squirrel had finished, it ran on to the next tree and Zee immedi-ately returned. He squatted down as if to incubate and as if he were not certain that another tragedy had struck. A few minutes later he stepped from the nest and departed.

Poor Zee and Naida were not put upon by fate. Rather they were suffering the same joys and heartaches or tragedies that are the lots of most wildlife, especially wild doves and pigeons. Most of their losses are from nat-ural causes, such as wind or predators. Some animals, like the Passenger Pigeons (Zee and Naida's larger cousins), are assailed by the hand of man, with the loss of eggs, ju-veniles, and adults by massive hunting and trapping. The Passenger Pigeon was one of the most abundant birds the world has ever known, yet more than a billion were killed in thirty years for the restaurant trade. The bird was gone, extinct early in this century.

The will to help young survive can be very strong. At a farmyard near town, where Zee and Naida sometimes fed, a pair began building in a Silver Maple at three meters. Since it was early in July, this was probably their second or third effort for the season. The male was an ardent builder and brought dry grass, which he placed before his mate who dutifully worked it into the nest. Only he didn't know when to stop. All during incubation, before he took his turn on the eggs, he continued bringing grass until the quarters became a large, loose structure resembling that of a House Sparrow. One of the two nestlings that hatched late in July became entangled in the mass of grass. The bird man found it alive when he came by and, upon packing down the pile, he found a third egg that had slipped to the bottom. Both chicks thrived for five more days until a gust of wind tipped out the unwieldy pile. One youngster survived the fall and at mid-day the male was brooding it on the ground. A corn cultivator stood unused beneath the tree and the bird-bander fashioned a nest of straw upon its seat, putting the baby in it. The parents found it there and raised it successfully without further incidents.

Occasionally, a pair of Mourning Doves will build a nest and successfully raise four families from it, while another pair may try time and again and raise but one family in a whole season. There is evidence that older birds have learned from experiences and are more successful at rearing their young. Usually a pair will try six or more times and rear three families.

The successes of friends of Zee and Naida illustrate this. In the chill of late April, one pair selected a homesite in a large Red Pine along a main street of town. It was on a horizontal branch six meters high and extending west four meters. This position received all of the heavy northwest and southwest winds of spring and sum-

mer. The first egg, laid on the second of May, hatched on
May 17; when the chicks were two and three days old, re-
spectively, their father almost knocked them from the tree
as he flushed wildly at some disturbance, but they crawled
back together. They fledged on May 30. Five days later, a
few more twigs were added to the nest and on the following day their mother laid. Both young hatched on June
18, and both celebrated the Fourth of July by fledging.
Immediately their parents renested, and the first egg of
the third brood was laid July 6. In fourteen days the eggs
hatched and the two hatchlings grew to sturdy youth, flying on August 4 when fifteen days old. At each brood the
nest had been augmented with grass and twigs until now it
appeared very unstable. But the ambitious owners added
more repairs on August 9 and laid egg number seven the
following day. For two weeks, the third pair of youngsters,
still under parental care, roosted in the tree not far from
the nest. Nestlings seven and eight hatched on August 24
and grew uneventfully to fly on September 9. Their parents flew with them to a nearby field where they rested
and fed for nearly a month while fall migrants of robins,
swallows, and doves threaded the sky by day, and the night
skies held bluebirds, warblers, and even a few ducks. Returning to town in October the pair began their fifth family
in the nest that was still recognizable. On October 12 an
early winter storm with cold rain and winds blew from the
northwest and continued to buffet the countryside for two
days. When the weather moderated the nest was broken
and an egg clung to it. Brood five had failed and their parents were on their way south. This one nest had been used
for five and a half months (May into October) and from it
eight juveniles had been sent out to face the world.

Zee and Naida's sixth nesting attempt for the year was
made in a small plum tree, built in a small fork only two
meters high. It was late in the season, almost the tenth of

September, and Naida was maturing her eggs a little more slowly than earlier in the year. The pair worked on the nest for two days and Naida's eleventh egg of the season was laid on the third day, followed by the twelfth egg two days later. This meant that the babies would hatch more than a day apart.

Even though Naida had agreed to build in this small plum tree, the limbs supporting it were too loosely interwoven, allowing the nesting material to gradually sink between the twigs. Recognizing this weakness, Zee began bringing one or two twigs or blades of grass each morning before he took his turn at incubation. After his morning preening he would have breakfast, drink, and upon returning to the nest, stop near it to pick up building material. Even with the slippage and loosening, the birds were able to hold it together and strengthen it. Zee continued this until the young were half grown.

When these birds were six days old, the man came to band them. As he walked under the tree the older bird, Haw-he (as doves are known by the Pima Indians) jumped in fear and as she fell, struck a sharp piece of bark along the tree trunk, tearing her food distended breast. The man banded her and returned her to the nest. It was Naida who first returned following this disturbance, for Zee had staggered away, faking a broken wing and then running along in front of this man as he walked away. As she stepped into the nest, Naida examined her young and saw Ha-he's injury. While she brooded over the little one, she carefully picked at the wound removing bits of bark, torn feathers, and dirt. This served to cleanse it and six days later, as Haw-he prepared to leave the nest, her wound had healed so that only an irregularity in the feathers marked its location.

October set in with cold rains and winds and nearly freezing temperatures for the first week. Most of the doves in this vicinity had finished raising their last families and had left for the south, but Zee and Naida, even with their desire to leave, stayed close to these two babies who did not want to try their wings because of bad weather. It was the fifteenth day before they could be induced to leave the nest. Zee and Naida spent another day teaching them what to eat and then flew with them to a woods not far from town. There they were left to fend for themselves as their parents winged toward Mexico. These last two were females, whereas the first four of this year's brood had been males.

CHAPTER FOUR
Haw-He and
Wa-ba-mi-mi

*T*HESE youngsters, Haw-he and Wa-ba-mi-mi (Chippawa for dove), were not alone, for other doves both young and old were present. Some of these, as young as themselves, had been left by their parents; others were from farther north and even some of the adults were local. They all remained in the vicinity of the woods because of an abundant food supply. They formed a little band of about thirty and could usually be found in hemp thickets along a stream that wound through the woods. When the winter snows set in, this band roosted on the north side of the creek under the embankment or beneath the roots of an overturned tree. They had several such roosts along the creek. If disturbed from one they would spend the night in another. A fox raided one of these roosts one night and captured the bird sleeping nearest the outer edge.

The morning sun warmed the birds before they left the streamside each day to fly a regular route to their feeding places. When the weather became so cold that the stream froze solid, they obtained water by eating snow. One bitterly cold night in January, Wa-ba-mi-mi could not keep her feet warm and her toes froze. Later she lost them, leaving her stub-footed, with only one or two perfect toes on each foot, leaving recognizable tracks in mud or soft snow. On this day that was so cold in the north, Zee and Naida were feeding with a large band of doves on weed seeds at the edge of a forest thicket in a low valley among the mountains of southern Mexico.

When winter released its grip upon forest and stream, Wa-ba-mi-mi moved to a nearby farm, where she met a sturdy young male who was singing vigorously from the roof of a barn. Like most farmyards of the Midwest, it was well populated by House Sparrows. These little ruffians nest in barns, eaves, water spouts, or almost any place where they can thrust a pile of straw. A pair had selected a tangle of branches in a Box Elder tree and had energetically woven straw among the twigs to form a disorderly bundle which they did not complete or use as a nest. Wa-ba-mi-mi's mate favored the top of this pile of hay and convinced her that it was a good place for a family. They began this family on May 28 and the two chicks hatched in their haystack and left safely on June 25. Their parents were back in three days, packed the hay down a little more and repaired the structure, but not sufficiently to hold the sparrow-built pile together. All went well for the doves, as oblivious as sharecroppers to the disheveled state of their home, or unable to do anything about it. When the youngsters were nearly fledging age, the house slowly disintegrated in a breeze. As the last of the straws loosened and fell away, the alert dovelets stepped on to the supporting limbs and watched their nest collapse. There they remained for two days before leaving with Wa-ba-mi-mi to join their father.

Haw-he left her sister and the streamside with the first spring thaws. She found a mate within the flock and their ardor was intense. Both were inexperienced in nest building and protection and they selected a small fork high in an Elm that was bare and exposed to the wind. A spring blizzard struck on April 14, piling wet snow along the limbs and nearby roofs. Haw-he wore a canopy of snow equally as great, for she was incubating during the predawn hours of snowfall. In spite of their valiant effort, a subsequent storm threw the nest and it's occupants from the tree.

Still using poor judgment of a site, they tried again, this time in a half-dead Silver Maple, building in a crotch of dead limbs ten meters above the ground. Not a particle of shade protected the nest or its occupants from hot summer suns and nothing covered it from the view of marauders. One nestling successfully fledged early in July and three days later Ha-he added a few twigs brought by her mate and they were renesting. Again, they were undisturbed and these young flew a month later. It was August 10 when a wind, riding before a squall, snapped a limb above the nest that fell and lodged upon it. Haw-he and her mate persisted and rebuilt, using this broken limb as a foundation, as well as the original fork. Two days later another wind blew the fragment free, carrying the nest with it. Still they persisted and rebuilt on location as before. On August 19, the eggs were destroyed by some predator, so they abandoned their efforts and went away.

Following this first season of erratic success, both birds joined migrating flocks and overwintered far to the south. Haw-he found a second mate for her second breeding season farther north in Iowa. Again she had but little success, raising only one brood during the entire five months of activity. Discouraged, she left her homeland and flew rapidly south early in September, arriving in the State of Jalisco on October 1, having averaged 60 miles a day over the entire 1,600 miles. Two days later, hunters from Guadalajara City intercepted Haw-he as she dropped to a streamside for her evening drink. She was 840 days old.

CHAPTER FIVE

Ha-wo Meets
Stump Face

THREADING their way through an open pecan and
oak forest of northern Texas flew a thin stream of doves.
As they passed a farm pond, several broke from the flock
and alighted at the water's edge. Shining metal gleamed
from the leg of one, Ha-wo. He drank, picked up a few
snails and pebbles, then rose to the limb of a nearby tree.
In a moment or two he was away, joining the ever-passing
parade. High in the blue sky throngs of swallows passed by
the thousands each hour. Alternating with bands of doves
were those of robins. It was August. It was not quite clear
to Ha-wo how it happened, but he had lost Wa-u-ia-uk in
a large flock of doves some time ago.

Several days later in Mississippi, many miles to the east, Wa-u-ia-uk was still with that flock. They had been lazily traveling southward finding choice fields of cowpeas and patches of delicious doveweed to feed on. Before them a hundred acres of the fertile land had been planted in cowpeas, planted early so that the pods would be ripe and brittle, shedding the peas at the time that migrating doves would be arriving from the north. Hundreds came each day to feed and then it was September 1.

Before dawn, men and women began arriving, parking their cars at a lot provided and joining others who had arrived earlier and camped for the night. Around the great field were numbered stakes marking the locations assigned to each shooter. Shooters paid their fees and were driven to their locations provided with a sun-shading umbrella, comfortable chairs, an icebox of cold drinks, ammunition, and spare guns if needed. During the day a pickup truck would drive around the periphery of the field, replenishing drinks and providing snacks and shells as needed.

Half an hour before sun up, Wa-u-ia-uk, joined by hundreds of others, swept into the field to feed and the carnage began. Shooting continued all day long until sunset as the fast-flying, confused, and terrified birds rushed into and out of the area, Wa-u-ia-uk falling with the hundreds of others. His mother in Iowa was quietly incubating another family, unaware of the tragedy that had struck down one of her sons. Periodically, the shooting was stopped, the dead birds gathered and distributed among those enjoying this "sport" so that none had more than his or her daily bag limit.

At hundreds of other places across the southland, hunters participated in such shoots, some smaller, some larger, many not so well organized, but all designed to kill as many birds as possible and to sharpen the shooters' skill.

Ha-wo saw many of his comrades fall at drinking pools and peafields, and had learned to avoid with all the speed of his powerful wings those places where he saw humans. After he crossed the Rio Grande he noticed a change in both the people and the land. There were fewer men armed with "talking sticks," but he had to avoid boys with sling shots as he flew down valleys ever southward. Finally, he passed a great city like those he had seen far to the North, then turned westward through mountain passes into a dry valley along a rushing river. Here the flock paused to fly no farther. They were in the State of Jalisco.

Ha-wo spent the winter here but not in the same valley as his father and mother. In the fall he had somewhat indifferently followed the migrating flocks southward. Now that the late winter days were lengthening, he again felt the urge to travel, but with no ultimate destination before him. Valleys and hills, rivers and forests, farmlands and cities, all passed as each day the flocks flew northward. Winter had yielded before them and the birds that stopped off along the way were those that had been there before and were seeking old territories or environments. Having no such place memories, Ha-wo was more interested in finding a mate than in his surroundings. But one day, as the flock flew over southern Iowa, the scene began to look familiar. Then he realized that this was the village where he had been raised. It was already April, and he had tried to claim a territory at several recent stops, only to find that the places that looked good to him were already occupied by males who vehemently hurried him on. Maybe he could do better here. He selected a garden and yard with large maple and cottonwood trees and several elms. A broken limb offered a place for observation and cooing. The site proved to be unoccupied, its previous owner having been struck by a car in Oklahoma.

Ha-wo began calling from his sentinel post, only to be immediately answered and challenged by a deep basso from his neighbor to the north. Ha-wo flew to the challenge only to stop and stare. His neighbor, who would eventually share this garden with him, was a large dove, but he had no face.

"No, to be exact," Ha-wo thought, "he has eyes and cheeks all right, but he has no bill." Only two rounded lumps at the level of the nostrils showed where his bill had been. "Stump Face," Ha-wo immediately labeled him.

He had not been "Stump Face" on that day months before when he and his migrating fellows swooped into a peafield in southern Texas for the abundance of food spread about, only to be met by a hail of lead pellets from a row of shooters stationed about the field. A searing blow in the face knocked him from the sky and he fell unconscious into a tangle of nettles. He lay there bleeding, his whole face torn apart, upper and lower mandibles and tongue carried away, while the hunters tramped by, looking for more targets. Regaining consciousness later, he crawled deeper among the nettles until hunger and thirst drove him from the hideout. His greatest need was water to replace all that his body had lost. His throat muscles still worked and he could suck up water, but picking up seeds was painful and nearly impossible. Remaining within short flights of water, he continued to search for food. It was everywhere and nowhere. With his face torn and beak missing, he could not grasp a seed. Slowly, day by day, he was starving. By turning his head he was finally able to grasp a seed or two at the corners of his mouth. Healing in all wild things is rapid, and the raw wounds soon scabbed over. In spite of pain and awkwardness, he learned to pick up enough seeds and kernels to keep alive. Winter came, but he was already far enough south to survive the occasional frost or cold night. By the advent of spring migration he had regained his weight and had healed his wounds, which left him beakless save for the rounded nubbins. He returned to his Iowa homeland as "Stump Face" and successfully raised several families with a wife he found there.

Ha-wo was an apathetic homemaker. He usually found wives among the returning females but rarely remained with them for long. One summer they built in an elm near the home of the bird-bander. Ha-wo was captured in a trap and, to distinguish him from other banded birds, his tail was dipped into merthiolate to stain it bright red. There was an aviary at the bird-bander's house and Ha-wo came each morning and evening to feed upon seeds spilled by captive birds. When he brought young on July 25, he led them to the porch to eat, but his wife was never seen there. On August 1, they re-nested in the same nest, and his irresponsibility as a father was evident to the birdman. He rarely appeared for his duty of incubation before 10 a.m. After the young hatched, he was even more irregular in his ministrations. Sometimes he fed the nestlings at nine o'clock; other times he did not come to them until noon, but he was usually present in the afternoons. Although rarely found farther than 50 meters from the nest; where he drank was not apparent. When this August family flew, he did not bring them to the porch to feed, but fed there himself three mornings, then joined the passing flocks.

In a nearby Norway Spruce, robins had built a nest in May and successfully fledged four youngsters. Soon after these had flown, Stump Face and his mate found and commandeered the empty bowl. She laid eggs in it by June 10, and they fledged one young on July 6. What happened during the following month Ha-wo did not know, but they were back in the spruce in August. The old robin nest had disintegrated in a rain storm, but Stump Face built a new nest on its foundation and he and his mate raised a pair of young males, which flew on August 28. During their juvenile training they returned to the spruce each evening to spend three nights there, but their father insisted that they leave, since their mother was busy with a new clutch, having had only five days of rest intervening since caring for them. When six days old the youngsters had been banded 38-356250 and 38-256266. Within a few days of leaving their home territory, they joined with other doves flying south. Outside of Stillwater, Oklahoma, the flock wheeled into the evening sun to drop by a stream, but swept back in confusion as gunfire erupted. Number 38-356250 was among those picked up by the retrievers; he was only 45 days old. On this day back in Lewis, Iowa, 450 miles to the north, two sisters waited impatiently at the nest as Stump Face and their mother came to feed them. Soon they too joined the flight south to thread the gauntlet of danger.

Young doves face a wide and uncertain world.

CHAPTER SIX

Zee and Naida
More Years Together

MOST of the doves that overwintered in the State of
Jalisco arrived after the autumn equinox, but the sun was
still almost directly overhead and it was hot. Life here
seemed far less hazardous to Zee than it had been in Iowa.
The river that they frequented was the Rio Grande de
Santiago and the land was not as intensively farmed as
in the North, permitting an abundance of wild plants to
grow, and offering a variety of seeds. With no superhigh-
ways and mostly gravel roads, automobiles were less of a
hazard, but North American hawks also wintered in these
mountains and some of the men here had guns, so the

doves still had to be cautious. Lazy days turned into lazy weeks and the birds fed, lounged, and slept. It became cooler and rained more as the sun moved on south below the equator until the shortest day, December 22.

As the earth moved along its great orbit, the sun began its northern trek and the days imperceptibly became longer. The overwintering birds began to feel an inward urge to move north with the warming isotherms. Slowly at first, small groups of doves filtered their way through valleys and among the small fields of the Mexican farmers. All across the continent from Southern California through Texas to Florida, great hosts of migratory birds also responded to this surge of spring and turned their eyes and thoughts to the North. Zee and Naida were among them and, although they occasionally saw each other, paid little attention to their former mate. They had become separated on the long trek to Iowa, where they had nested and known home the summer before.

Zee came into his small village first and went directly to his old territory, but it was already occupied by an earlier arrival, possibly one of the birds that had overwintered locally. One of Zee's alternate territories had been near two large spruce trees and a large pine in the front yards of two houses. Favored because the trees had such splendid flat limbs, perfect for holding and concealing nests, many males competed for these trees. Competition was even keener this year because one of the homeowners had cut down the large pine.

Zee cooed and growled at other males that coveted his bit of homeland, even engaging in loud wing slapping contests on fences, wires, and rooftops where he and his opponents faced and slapped each other until one gave way.

Lack of trees may force doves to use **eaves troughs** as nest sites.

Zee held his place until one day Naida joined him, having heard and recognized his strong coo when she entered the village. Since the pine tree was missing, some substitute must be found. Zee thought he had it: the end of an eaves trough at the top of the house which stood behind the forlorn tree stump. Naida thought it was a good location and they nearly filled the end of the trough with a sturdy pile of twigs. Both had forgotten spring and summer thunderstorms and overlooked what could happen at such a homesite. And it did! A heavy May shower filled the trough to overflowing. As it was afternoon, Zee was on duty incubating a pair of eggs and he kept his post amidst lightning, thunder, and a deluge of rain, with his head held high to keep from drowning. Amazingly enough, the submergence did not damage the eggs, and he and Naida brought up two healthy young before the next flooding shower.

Such torrential summer storms in the Midwest often brought death in a different form. Fortunately, Zee and Naida survived this one, but the occupants of a nearby home six meters up in a Silver Maple did not. Nestlings were a week old when thunderheads rolled overhead and great hail stostones up to ten centimeters in diameter fell for several minutes, followed by heavy rain. A six-centimeter piece of ice struck this nest a direct blow, knocking it apart and killing the brooding male as well as the two young. Not far away another direct blow knocked out both young, killing one. The other was severely wounded about the eyes, head, and back, but crawled into a garage to escape the torrential rain. Found by the bird-bander, it was nursed back to health, banded, and released.

During another brood attempt that summer, Zee and Naida nested in an apple tree. The man still came by to put shiny rings on the legs of their babies. This time the limb broke beneath his weight. Nest, young, and man all fell to the ground. One of the young was killed by the fall; the other the man took and raised as a pet. That bird had many experiences such as falling into a dish of gravy, trying to eat ice, and learning the taste and delight of butter, but these are other stories.

In July Zee thought he had a good location for their third nest of that season. It was, of all places, on the top of a Fox Squirrel nest, high in an elm tree. Fortunately the squirrels had moved. Zee and Naida raised two families there in July and August before departing to the South. Early one morning in August, a Screech Owl, having completed its night of cruising, landed on a limb within a meter of Naida. She was dismayed, but did not move. The doves continued in their nest duties, while the owl dozed there the whole day and then flew on with dusk.

In reciprocation, squirrels liked the location of a nest of another pair of doves and used it for the foundation upon which they built their own. And in the worst of judgment, doves tried twice to nest on top of an active squirrel nest, losing their eggs each time the squirrels came home.

Zee and Naida never again spent the winter together in the South, but for five years they mated and raised more babies in Lewis, Iowa. Each winter Zee returned to the valleys of Jalisco without his mate in the same flock.

$\mathcal{I}$T was not far north of the Rio Grande in the beautiful Big Bend country. A mottled, tawny bobcat tom lounged on an oak limb in the late afternoon sun outside of his daytime retreat. This was a termite-enlarged cavity in the bole, left by a fallen limb. Although it was almost evening, he was not hungry, but it was time to forage. He dropped from his limb to move with exquisite feline stealth among the coverts of the mesquite shrubs toward a nearby stream where he might quench his thirst before more serious hunting.

For several days Naida had been moving north at a leisurely pace. It was March and, although the White-winged Doves from coastal slopes along the way had been nesting in individual pairs or gathering in flocks for their colonial nesting, she felt no urgency to hurry on. She knew Zee would be there when she arrived at her destination.

Beautiful valleys of southern Mexico, winter haven for many North American Mourning Doves.

Naida crossed the Rio Grande after midday and noticed a small glade by a wooded tributary north of this great river. She had not eaten since morning and it looked an inviting place to stop before finding a roost for the night. She slid silently through the woodland and dropped by the stream. There she found palatable seeds in abundance, even though wintering birds, mice and other rodents had fed there all winter.

As the bobcat moved toward the stream on silent pads, a dove sped above him and landed near the water. He halted in attention behind a clump of thistles. Unaware of her danger the dove fed toward him, almost enough fh for a strike. But she turned away and found seeds at some distance, then worked back. Eyes glowing and in quivering anticipation the feline waited. A long, pointed ear twitched at a buzzing fly. Catching this slight movement Naida rose on screaming wings. With a prodigious leap the predator pulled her down.

Zee waited.

CHAPTER SEVEN
Later Years

ZEE's sixth year was a good one. He and the mate that replaced Naida had again escaped the rigors of hunting and migration. Spring in the Midwest was bursting with enthusiasm and vitality as they entered Lewis and sought out old haunts. Crocuses, violets, Dutchman's Breeches, and Spring Beauties were blooming. Earthworms were mating and the cardinals, doves, and frogs in nearby ponds were filling the air with song. Box-Elder trees and elms were in full bloom. A returning Eastern Phoebe was hawking dancing midges from the air.

As April wore on, in spite of recurrent cold snaps, robins were building their sturdy nests and laying their sky-blue eggs. Chipping Sparrows had a nest in a small Blue Spruce. House Martins were courting with aerobatics; hyacinth, apple and apricot trees were in full bloom;

grackles were building new nests and House Sparrow youngsters were already hatching. A late-arriving Brown Thrasher was in full song.

May entered with a cardinal nest of four eggs in a porchside vine. An abundant hatch of June Beetle larvae in lawns provided a rich harvest of white grubs for the robins. As one dug for them, House Sparrows harassed it until it dropped the unearthed grub, which they in turn snatched up and carried to a nest of hungry youngsters. This did not seem to perturb the robin; it put up little resistance, quickly plucked forth another grub and carried it up to its own nestlings.

Elm seeds ripened and were shed in a thin green rain. Bluejays were nest building or harassing other species, in one case driven away from a nest of robins by irate parents. Young Fox Squirrels and House Sparrows had already left their nests while catbirds built theirs; grackles were on eggs, and a Brown Thrasher couple lost their eggs to a squirrel.

In the latter half of May a crow wrested a struggling fledgling from a robin family and flew off with five robins in futile pursuit. A baby squirrel fell from its nest in a hollow maple to the concrete sidewalk beneath. Stunned, it lay there while its mother stood beside it until it revived enough to be led back up the tree. A grackle watched a flicker dig up a white grub, knocked the flicker from its feet and purloined the grub. The Chipping Sparrow nest in the Blue Spruce had three speckled eggs when a Brown-headed Cowbird removed one and laid her own larger one there. One Chipping Sparrow hatched along with the cowbird, but did not survive as the tiny sparrows struggled to raise the interloper.

June arrived with new life at full throttle. So many trees about town had been removed during the winter that the lack of habitual nest sites forced eleven pairs of doves to use eaves troughs on nearby houses. Seven of these families were successful. Hatching spiders were ballooning, filling the summer air with their floating webs. Catalpa was in its full, gorgeous bloom and young grackles were fledging, some to drown in a heavy June rain. Blood-red Box-Elder Bug nymphs had hatched and the air was filled with the snow of blowing and floating cottonwood seeds.

By the end of June, families of Screech Owls had outgrown their tree hollows and solemn-faced youngsters sat in court along limbs, waiting for darkness and their suppers, three in one family, five in another. Robins were feeding their second broods and Brown Thrashers had already fledged.

July found a pair of kestrels aggressively protecting a team of youngsters learning to fly and hunt clicking grasshoppers. By now most bird families had flown or were under parental training to prepare them for survival. A late family of Loggerhead Shrikes was with young, supplied with many large insects and an occasional birdlet. Barn Swallow and House Martin families were roosting on wires and gathering in flocks to harvest aeroplankton from above ripening fields of corn or alfalfa as they prepared to leave for the tropics. The Chipping Sparrow couple had succeeded in raising a family without the intervention of the cowbirds. Hot summer breezes rang with the cacophonous singing of cicadas emerging from the husk-like nymphs that crawled up tree trunks and walls. A young bluejay tried unsuccessfully to steal one of the singers from the clutches of a Red-headed Woodpecker, but was driven off by the indignant woodpecker.

All of these and more Zee and Mate Two watched as they raised family after family of their own and led them to feeding and watering places and taught them to avoid cats and dogs, cars and undisciplined children. From his nest Zee watched one tragic tableau which oppressed him for several days. A passing car struck a Fox Squirrel hurrying across the street and broke its back. With both hind legs paralyzed and a deep gash across its back, it hauled itself hand over hand across the street to the base of a Silver Maple tree. Then, in obvious agony, it struggled in the same manner up to a low limb. When someone approached it continued hand over hand up the tree from limb to limb to its den nearly ten meters above and crawled in to die there in misery.

With four different loves during the next five years, Zee experienced many housing and family problems. His experience with Naida and three eggs served him one spring when he selected a small fork of limbs five meters up in a Box-Elder. He and his mate had been hasty and the nest was flimsy, having taken only two days, May 6 and 7, for completion. But his wife was urgent and laid on May 8 and again on May 9 and 10. Three eggs can tax the incubating abilities of a pair, but she and Zee were both large and healthy, hatching their family in 16 days, consecutively on May 24, 25, and 26. The last was, of course, the runt, considerably smaller than the other two; but he held his head up enough and peeped for food along with his nestmates. This time there was enough to go around. A week later the runt had caught up with the other two. The three so crowded the nest that heads and tails seemed to point in all directions. From the ground Zee could be seen balanced on top of them to keep them warm. With so much weight and scrambling the nest began to disintegrate. On June 9, as twigs fell away, the three youngsters stepped off the nest and onto the limb. They were two weeks old. Three days later they joined Zee in a nearby tree. One of them was Paloma.

CHAPTER EIGHT
Paloma

$\mathcal{T}$HEY stayed with their father near the nest site for a week as he showed them what to eat, where there was water, and how to avoid cats and dogs. Zee taught by demonstration and voice. He picked up seeds that were palatable and dropped them, and the fledglings ate them. He led the youngsters to water. If a cat approached, he voiced a warning note and flew at a distance of safety. Dogs were less of a hazard, the warning note was slightly different, and the escape distance much shorter. All of these lessons the young learned by duplicating their father's actions.

Hawks? There wasn't much that he could recommend about protection from hawks, except eternal vigilance. Juveniles could learn by watching other birds and listening to their warning calls if a hawk appeared. They might meet the Prairie Falcon. It was fast, but they could outfly it! The big hawks with broad wings were slow and easy to escape, but they rarely attempted a strike on doves. The Merlin was another fast one, but, like the Prairie Falcon, they would see it most often down south during the winter. Also in fall and winter months they would have to look out for the Sharp-shinned and Cooper's Hawks. Both of these would hide in trees or shrubs to waylay a dove or other bird, but if you saw them you could outfly them. Because it was larger and stronger, the Cooper's Hawk was the more dangerous of the two. Then there was the Peregrine Falcon, most dangerous of all! A dove was bound to lose if it attempted to outfly it! The only way for a dove to escape was to dive into the ground and flatten itself. This was effective because the Peregrine swooped with such speed that if it struck the ground it would break its legs, so it had to pull out of a dive just above the dove. "But," thought Zee, "it's been years since I saw a Peregrine. Maybe they are gone like the Passenger Pigeons I once heard of."

What about cars? There was little Zee could show his offspring about cars. Escaping an approaching vehicle was a matter of judging its speed. If a young bird misjudged and was struck, it did not survive to learn more. Because of the dove's need for grit in its gizzard, gravel roads are very popular sources of sharp pebbles. This is especially true in farming areas where there is but little sand. In Nebraska the bird-bander found 1,600 birds of 56 species killed along roadsides, a high percentage of these along gravel roads, or those paved with "black-top" and bordered by gravel. Among these victims were 55 Mourning Doves. Other species suffered heavily as well: 386 Ring-necked Pheasants, 183 Red-headed Woodpeckers, 109 Prairie Horned Larks, 95 Western Meadowlarks, and 93 Burrowing Owls. All of the bird mortalities were highest in July, August, and September when the greatest number of juveniles were present and had not yet learned to judge the speed of cars. More than half of all of the doves seen along roadsides were noted there in July and August and 75% of those killed by passing cars were found in these months as well. This relationship was found to be true for other species. Zee could only hope that his families would learn to avoid speeding cars.

Following this training all three youngsters wandered off and fed in the fields with others of similar age. The summer passed and sometime in August flocks began moving south. Paloma joined them and flew with great swiftness.

Nicaragua is a land not much greater in area than Iowa, nestled in Central America between two cordillera mountain ranges with many volcanic peaks. Between these two verdant ranges lie two beautiful lakes, Lake Managua and the 100-mile long Lake Nicaragua, encompassing 3,000 square miles of water. Paloma arrived along the shores of Lake Nicaragua, among the farms that bordered it, sometime in October. Political strife in this country placed guns in the hands of most men and boys and any moving target became a challenge. Paloma fell before a 14-year-old shooter on November 19, only five months old and more than 2,000 miles from home; the farthest known of the bird-bander's baby doves.

A year later one of Paloma's brothers found a mate in an orchard on a farm a mile or so from town. The pair successfully raised two families among the apple trees and in July had built a third nest on a horizontal limb at four meters, a location similar to the others. In mid-July one egg was already being incubated along with another, which, upon closer inspection, was a very pale blue. A Yellow-billed Cuckoo had crept into the nest when both parents were absent and laid this one.

The cuckoo is a slim grayish-brown with light underparts and a down-curved, yellow bill. Another casual builder like the doves, it puts only a few twigs together before laying, and occasionally uses the nests of other species. Belonging to a great pandemic family of birds, cuckoos throughout the world include an unbelievable pantheon of shapes, sizes, and colors. Some are parasitic, most are not. Our almost mythical bird of animated cartoons, the roadrunner, belongs to this family. North American species are not parasitic, but occasionally Yellow-billed Cuckoos get careless and lay in other households. Its incubation is shorter than that of the Mourning Dove.

Nine days after the nest was discovered by the bird-bander, it contained two dove eggs and a newly-hatched, tiny, black individual with black pinfeathers and a yellow bill. But cuckoos are insect-eaters and pigeon milk was inadequate for this tiny vagrant, which quickly starved. The presence of this foreigner delayed development in the dove eggs, which did not hatch until the 16th day, and these chicks also were ill-fated. Some predator attacked them and their mother at night when they were a week old. It is easy to suspect that owls might do this, but so few remains of doves have been found in owl pellets that this is doubtful. The domestic cat and raccoon are always suspect. Feathers on the ground about the tree often support the accusation that a mammalian predator was the culprit.

The father returned to his early morning duties aware that his mate had not called. Sorrowfully he examined the shattered nest and turned away. By mid-morning a Yellow-billed Cuckoo was surreptitiously pilfering usable material from the forlorn nest. Possibly it was the parent of the little black nestling.

CHAPTER NINE

The Storm

ONE of Zee's daughters, Turtura, in searching for a mate, had moved fifty miles north to find both a mate and a home in the little town of Portsmouth. Like her father's home territory, it was a farm community no larger than Lewis, surrounded by fields of corn. There were a few business houses, a town square and a park of about an acre shaded by Box-Elder trees and American Elms. Business men and retired farmers had neat frame homes surrounded by white picket fences and green lawns screened by shade trees and shrubs. Most homes had flower or vegetable gardens as well.

Like Lewis, Portsmouth also supported an abundance of wildlife. This was Turtura's second year here and she and her mate had a nest in one of the Box-Elder trees of the park. It was the ninth of July and nature had been kind, so the village was full of nests, young birds, and mammals.

The night was more than half gone when Turtura huddled closer over her two downy youngsters, protecting them from a gusty rain that had been falling since midnight. Suddenly the rain and wind ceased and she felt anguish in her ears from an abrupt reduction in barometric pressure. In vague uneasiness she cringed lower as a great roaring began. It ascended in volume like the approach of massive locomotives and a tornado was upon them. It swept in from the northwest, a screaming banshee of indescribable voices. Houses exploded, trees were ripped from their roots, Turtura was slammed against a wall and fell unconscious amidst its torn timbers, somewhat protected there from the torrential rain and hail that drowned many unfortunates not yet killed by the wind. It took only moments to devastate the entire environment and two hours to drown and beat it to a pulp.

Dawn gradually revealed utter desolation. No bird called, no wind, no rustling of leaves, only an intense silence, just the quiet of death. Turtura tried to move from her place beneath the fallen wall and found that, badly bruised, she could fly awkwardly to the nearby stub of a shattered Box Elder. Around her it was a scene as of winter, worse than winter. No leaves upon the trees, only bruised and shattered limbs, and the ground was covered with vegetable debris. A nearby cornfield was merely wretched stubble. Grass was beaten down, vegetables in gardens pulled up; onions, radishes and beets lay around, flower gardens stripped with only torn petals on the dejected grass.

Every building in town had been damaged. Stores were leveled by the screaming wind, followed by hail and five inches (12 cm) of torrential rain. The basement of a home was filled full with hail and leaves blown in through a stripped door. The town was on a southeast-facing slope and the tornado struck from the northwest, riding in from the surrounding plains where it struck a brick church, school, and parsonage at the brow of the hill. The church steeple was demolished and walls stressed, school windows blasted in, but these buildings deflected the wind from the parsonage, which suffered less. The savage wind swept above the town's residences and dipped into the business district, demolished stores and the park and then moved on southeast.

Since such winds whirl counterclockwise most of the felled trees fell westward. The deciduous trees were almost entirely stripped of foliage, but evergreen trees showed less damage, although some were uprooted.

There was the stillness of death; no living thing moved except people and their pets. The light increased and among the leaves below Turtura a toad struggled forth. House Sparrows began to chatter about a leaning barn; a Red-Headed Woodpecker peeked out from its nesthole in a Box Elder and ventured forth. Other doves had survived and a House Wren sang near its tilted, but intact nest box. Twenty Chimney Swifts had survived the drenching in some chimney or had flown in from the less severly damaged countryside. A wing-crippled robin walked among the debris and an Eastern Kingbird flew to a shattered treetop. In all the town, other than the sparrows, only 37 birds survived.

Scattered among the detritus before her, Turtura could see the torn bodies of nine bluejays, 17 Mourning Doves, six House Sparrows, six Common Grackles, four Baltimore Orioles, including two beautiful males, four robins, three young Screech Owls from a tree hollow ripped open by the wind, one Northern Flicker, two Eastern Kingbirds, two Red-headed Woodpeckers, and one forlorn Downy Woodpecker, 55 in all.

In the school yard and about the church were 150 more bodies, including rabbits, Red Bats, and Fox Squirrels. Turtura could not know this but more than 5,000 beautiful creatures had been destroyed in a scant few moments.

Townspeople moved about, surveying their losses and the storm damage, cleaning and repairing where repairs seemed warranted, and picking up the sad remains. Where House Sparrows had been sleeping in a clump of willows there were now 108 bodies, but of all the birds, the sparrows roosting in buildings fared the best. Other species suffered heavy losses: over 1,000 doves, nearly an equal number of robins, hundreds of bluejays and grackles, plus many of 15 other species.

But life forever survives and a week later the injured robin was still present. Birds from surrounding, less-damaged areas moved into the void and the trees were beginning to sprout new leaves. The surviving Red-headed Woodpeckers were caring for eggs or young, House Wrens had eggs or young in their houses, and the sparrows had built or were building new nests about broken buildings. A pair of orioles had woven their pendulous nest in the top of a maple tree, and there were dove nests in a spruce and a White Pine tree, each nest with eggs.

Two weeks later there were four Red-headed Woodpecker nests, five wren families, ten sparrow nests and two of the orioles. A starling was carrying food to young that had survived and a robin's nest contained three eggs. There were 13 pairs of doves, Turtura among them, that had found mates or acquired new ones, but half of these nests were again destroyed by a heavy squall on July 29.

On the last day of July there were three robin nests with thriving young, the last of which were fledged later in August. By that time most of the doves had stopped attempting to nest and joined the migrating flocks that began appearing at the end of the month. Now much of the town had been repaired and the deciduous trees bore new leaves. Next year new birds would find and move into the territories vacated by the storm losses and things would appear near normal again about the town and in the park.

CHAPTER TEN

Zee Meets
a Bat

IN that same year another daughter of Zee found a home to the west at a farmyard in central Nebraska. In this same farmyard a pair of Loggerhead Shrikes were building an April nest in an elm at about five meters. Six eggs had been laid by May 5 and all of the four chicks that hatched were raised, fledging on June 5. By July 1st, Zee's daughter and her husband had found and used this sturdy nest, their two young hatching in mid-July and fledging by August. In the meantime the shrikes had built a second nest in an adjoining elm. Another pair of doves also built in this tree, but their newly-hatched chicks disappeared, the shrikes being suspected of this assault. The shrikes raised three youngsters in this second brood which flew on

July 10. More doves moved in, but wind destroyed their efforts. Zee's daughter put the shrikes' first nest to use again in August, but failed when a squirrel ate the eggs in mid-incubation. By now the breeding season was late and both shrikes and doves turned to their flights south.

It was mid-June and Zee and Mate Three had selected a small fork of branches in an apple tree as their nest site, where he now sat quietly incubating two eggs. Always alert, he watched his surroundings. Beneath a leaf only a few feet above him was a round, brown object. As he watched, it slowly unfolded and scratched with a wing finger and quickly enfurled again. It was a Hoary Bat, one of many that had arrived in town in past weeks and was now using this leaf as a daily resting place.

With no further action, Zee lost interest, but just before he dozed off he saw it move again. This time it reversed itself. Clinging to the petiole with its wing fingers it lowered its body and defecated to avoid dirtying itself. It was in this exposed position that Zee could see four newly-born babies clinging to the female's breasts. As she grasped the leaf with her feet and returned to an inverted position, they continued to cling to her, now upside down. Zee watched during the day as the babies occasionally squirmed in her fur and she cleaned them with her tongue.

Zee missed most of the bat activity because he and Mate Number Three had changed places before sundown when the furry brown bat propelled herself into space with her juvenile load. He did not renew his nest duties until after the little mother had swept into the apple tree soon after dawn to cling to her leaf. These were insectivorous bats with greatly reduced eyes and great ears and nose leafs to compensate for the lack of vision. As darkness sets in they leave their individual roosts to feed for most of the night, often upon insects that swirl about street lights.

Each bat issues a sound so shrill that it is inaudible to the human ear. Echoes of this sound reflected from flying insects are directed by the large ear and nose-leaf lobes into the ears to focus the bat on its elusive prey. Each bat's call is recognized by its family and by others. Among bats that live in dense colonies in great caves, the cries of the young are distinguishable and recognizable to the returning mothers. Among those that roost singly, the use of calls is not so demanding. Each tiny mother who gives birth every spring carries her progeny as she flies the nocturnal corridors of woodland and field capturing moths, beetles, and other insects to renew her energies and provide milk for her passengers.

Zee noted that the young bats grew rapidly and within a week were almost as long as the mother's curled body. Gradually they gained weight and each succeeding sundown her flight became more labored. When the young were fifteen days old she could no longer support their combined weight and left them hanging under her leaf as she went off in search of supper. When dawn came and Zee's mate awakened, the little bat mother had already returned and her four healthy youngsters were clinging to or beside her. Sometime during the fourth or fifth week they flew off into the night with her, where she taught them how to hunt and fed them insects on the wing. In the morning light they might be clinging to separate leaves or again in a furry cluster. Now they were fully as large as she. One morning Zee noticed that there were only three present, two with the mother and one beneath an adjoining leaf. Then one of these did not return. Finally, by July 15, more than a month since Zee first noticed the family, they all departed, not to use the roost again. But by then Zee was busy with fledglings of his own.

CHAPTER ELEVEN

Mac

*E*ARLY in his tenth summer at Lewis, Zee sired a son, Mac, who was destined to lead an exceptional life. Soon after fledging, Mac left the confines of Lewis and joined small flocks of juveniles. He was always the excitable and inquisitive one and asked many questions of them. They came from the north, east, and west, but few from the south. As fall approached, they were joined by many birds from far north. They talked of the great plains and woodlands, many days to the north, and the plans of many of them to return to these homelands in the spring. Mac felt no affinity for any land. After all, his father had sent him away when his mother had started another family.

Mac and his friends were already far to the south and the ranks of his flock were increased by arriving adults. Time was unknown to the him, the days monitored only by hunger and thirst. But as the midday sun began to move closer to the zenith (the autumnal equinox), the adult birds that had joined them became nervous and alert. On a bright morning, September 1st, the land around Mac began to burst into roaring blasts and brilliant flashes and birds began to drop all around him. Terrified, he bolted into a thicket of mesquite. Day after day the shooting was repeated; on the sixth and seventh days (Saturday and Sunday), the blasts were heavier and more frequent. Mac lost friend after friend, but he became more efficient at spotting and avoiding the men with guns. Eventually survivors of the populations that nested from the western ocean to the continent's midlands found shelter in southern Mexico. Here they were subject to sporadic hunting all winter. Other populations overwintered around the Gulf of Mexico from Florida to Texas and on into southern California. Mac entered the State of Jalisco, unaware that his father was there ahead of him.

Mac met many doves from across America using these mountain valleys as winter havens. He even glimpsed birds from east of the great river. Among the flocks were birds from California. One of them, Huelota, was particularly attractive, a year older than Mac, but very dainty. Part of her appeal was that he could dominate her, but because she was older there was much to learn from her. Past the winter solstice the days began to lengthen and the birds' hormones were again triggered, stimulating them to move north, both to mate and to migrate. Soon the flocks were in movement, but many began to turn eastward and friends among these reminded Mac of his Iowa homelands. But having no territorial aspirations for Iowa, and a love for Huelota, he continued northward along the west coast of Mexico.

Dove hunting was occasional and usually avoidable, but there was no real peace until they crossed into California (where dove hunting season was closed). Soon they were in a big city, flying through a great park with grottoes and fields for wild animals, many different from creatures Mac had seen before. But what was most spectacular was the many thousands of doves that inhabited these lands. They fed among the exotic animals and drank from pools or streams. Mac learned that many had lived all their lives here. Others were from lands farther north.

In a few days he and Huelota moved north, but again they encountered a vast city, so vast that they could not see across it no matter how high they flew, partly because it was covered by a smog of smoke and evil-smelling gases. This city also harbored great numbers of Mourning Doves and they were introduced to a close relative, the Spotted Dove. There were many kinds of people in this great city; the Spotted Dove an immigrant among them. Its kind had been here for at least a quarter of a century. Larger than Mac and with a very different song, they were as abundant as the Mourning Dove in some neighborhoods. But, like the House Sparrows, Spotted Doves are not migrants and lived their whole lives in the city.

It was here Mac heard of a wonderful nesting place beyond the mountains to the north, an olive grove so large that there were thousands of trees and it was near both water and food, a tenement of species. A dove that he met in San Diego had mentioned that he was born there but now had his homeland along the Salton Sea to the east. Mac wondered about this place and its importance as a bird haven. He heard it was so crowded that only resident pairs returned to it year after year and new pairs could enter only when there was a vacancy. Huelota assured him it was where they were going. Her previous mate had been shot just outside of the grove. She hoped that Mac could carve out a holding for them.

During their flight over the mountains Mac met other doves who had been raised in the grove, but were now living in other parts of the state, some as far north as Ukiah, two to the east near a lake (Lake Isabella), some in San Bernardino County, some only five miles west of the grove near Shafter. He also learned of the breach of the grove's serenity every fall, when hunters descended upon it to kill many doves before they could migrate, even leaving nestlings to die without parents.

Mac and his friends arrived at the grove late in March to find the place teeming with activity. He selected a spreading olive tree toward the northern edge as his singing post, thereby beginning a daily singing and wing-slapping battle to retain his priority. The grove included 62 rows of 40 large, crowned olives, averaging 60 centimeters in trunk diameter. The low, flat, entwining limbs were ideal nesting sites. To the east a bulrush-filled irrigation ditch provided food and water and beyond it was pasture land. Grape arbors to the south and croplands to the west and north provided abundant weed seeds and insects for the hosts of birds that came to roost or nest in the grove. It was especially attractive to House Finches and by mid-spring nearly every one of the more than 2,500 trees supported a finch nest. The House Finches were of little concern to Mac and Huelota even though both they and the finches were seed eaters. The House Finches picked up and cracked smaller seeds, which they fed as gruel to their youngsters. The doves swallowed larger seeds without cracking them, having a gizzard to perform this chore and they fed their young pigeon milk as well as moistened seeds. Many male doves selected unused House Finch nests as foundations for their own and the resulting stability produced more fully-fledged young.

By early May, House Finch activity was at its peak with at least 800 nests of eggs or young. There were 150 dove nests as well. Mac was busy defending his holdings and helping Huelota with a pair of healthy youngsters. To his surprise, the same man that had banded his father in Iowa came to band his family here in the grove. Mac's "associates" in the grove included the families of 90 pairs of Bullock Orioles, 30 pairs of Black-Crowned Night Herons, 12 of robins, and 10 of House Sparrows. During June, many of the House Finches completed their family duties, but 330 finch nests remained active while dove pairs continued to pour in. Now there were 535 dove nests in the grove. In late August, just prior to the opening of the September hunting season, 77 dove families were still present.

To Mac, nesting at the olive grove was entertaining as well as challenging. Mourning Doves are solitary nesters, but often nest closely in a favored location. So it was here. Hundreds of pairs were using these wonderful resources. Mac and Huelota were raising family after family and Mac enjoyed his surroundings. In cities and at farmyards, a nest site was often located so as to offer little to see, but here in the grove there was continuous action.

From his nest high in the olive tree, Mac could watch the happenings in three House Finch nests beneath him. The nest to his north had been that of a robin. Only the foundation of last year's nest was still present when the finches found it. They rapidly built their sturdy, but somewhat unkempt nest upon it. The bright-red male was more of a nuisance than a help to his dull-colored, but ambitious wife, who laid egg after egg until there was a clutch of five. These she assiduously incubated and four tiny balls of fluff eventually hatched. Now the male, who had done little more than sing or accompany her to her feeding ground, where he pestered her with love-making, joined in feeding the nestlings. This was a process interesting to Mac, who swallowed seeds whole and regurgitated them with pigeon milk into the throats of his babies. The finches collected smaller seeds, each of which was carefully husked and the kernel swallowed. When back at the nest, these broken kernels, with digestive juices from the crop, were pumped into their babies. A similar action, but a different food.

These nestlings were as naked as Mac's newly-hatched, except for sparse, long, cottony down. Since the youngsters remained in the nest less than two weeks, this down was quickly replaced by mottled brown feathers. Getting these noisy and husky babies out of the nest for their first flight was tedious, and amusing to Mac as he watched.

To the south was another House Finch home and Mac had only to turn around to watch it. They had built in a fork of twigs and everything progressed normally until one morning there was much scolding and loud yelling. Mac opened his eyes to see what was the matter, and there below him a dark, gray-brown bird, larger than the finches was at the nest. Both finches were screaming and flying at it. A Brown-headed Cowbird female, it ignored this raucous objection and ate two of the eggs. Then it turned and laid a bright bluish egg in the nest and flew on as the male finch dashed at her. He continued to follow the Cowbird to the edge of his territory, while his mate returned to the eggs. She nestled upon them, but the disparity in sizes was disturbing to her. The cowbird egg was too big. It was late in the day and, as darkness approached, the nest still did not feel right, so she desisted and went to roost alone. Next morning she was back at the nest, where she began covering the eggs. Both she and her mate brought new material and she built another floor to the nest, covering both her eggs and that of the intruder. This was a strategy often used by House Finches to thwart cowbirds. In coming days she laid four more eggs and they raised four young happily. The man who put rings on birds banded them, and he later examined the nest to find the double floor and the unhatched Brown-headed Cowbird and finch egg.

However, this strategy was lacking in the beautiful Lark Sparrow. Mac could see a nest of this species on the ground at the base of a nearby Olive. The nest was artfully woven of plant fibers lined with horsehair and decorated on the outside with drying flowers of several plants. Here he saw the cowbird drive away the sparrow, exposing three, lovely, spotted eggs of grayish-blue. She removed one egg and deposited her own. Later the cowbird and one Lark hatched, but only the cowbird survived.

So the daily pageantry of life was all around Mac. As August slowly wore away, he began to hear comments among the doves drinking at the canal or feeding near it. "Finish and get out of here!" "The dangerous times begin soon when men come with guns to the canal and grove." "Leave, get out of here!"

Except for laggards among other species or pairs having nests late in the season, all of the species except the doves had finished their breeding. But almost all species of doves are designed for long breeding seasons. Many had moved on as they fledged their most recent young, but there were still 77 nests in the grove as September 1 broke with a beautiful, clear sunrise.

Mac and Huelota had just hatched their fifth brood. The bright Sunday morning was suddenly shattered by gunfire from all sides and Huelota, who had been dozing nearby, jumped up and fled. She had been through this before and the only survival was to seek the desert where you could see men approaching or find secret, small water holes. Mac had just fed his youngsters and crouched over them in terror. Some boys with light rifles or shotguns wandered through the grove shooting down the nests, but did not see Mac, who was high in the tree. The bird-bander came to the grove the next morning to walk slowly through it, grieving at the slaughter: a kestrel, a vulture, a robin, feathers of doves, dead adults or youngsters in the nests.

Mac rode out the whole day watching the uproar around him. It slacked off at sundown and he began to look for Huelota. She did not return. He fed the squirming nestlings, but he was a male and males are not programmed to care for nestlings at night. In confusion he responded to his old habits, left the nest, and roosted alone in his sleeping place in a nearby eucalyptus. The following dawn he returned to the nest to find the youngsters cold and barely alive. He brooded and worked with them all day, but the younger was dead by sundown. Again he could not spend the night at the nest, and on the second morning he found the older had succumbed. He worked with both, but there was no response and a nearby gunshot explosion sent him away.

With no Huelota and no juveniles to train, Mac joined the loose flocks flying south, dodging occasional hunters, on and on, back to Jalisco.

Winter passed, the sun climbed back into the northern hemisphere, and Mac returned to California. At the olive grove he was surprised to find Huelota already arrived. She had escaped the hunters. Year after year they returned to raise their families.

It was their eighth year at the grove. The morning, like most spring mornings in central California, was clear and warm. Huelota had just scolded Mac for arriving late for his nest duties, a much-repeated scolding. He was feeding the well-feathered youngsters when he heard the roar of heavy tractors and bulldozers rolling over the grove. Rapidly the grove began to disappear, and as tree after tree was wrenched from the soil and piled to be burned, nests and occupants were dashed aside. Mac's youngsters got away just two days before their tree fell and their displaced parents had to seek a new territory. The grove became a parking lot and the many species of birds using it had to seek homes at other locations. With so many territories vacated each year by the hunting season, it was not difficult for the displaced doves to find other nest locations. Mac and Huelota found one at a farmyard near the town of Shafter. It was much more difficult for resident species such as the finches, Night Herons, and Orioles, since habitats in the vicinity of the grove were already saturated with their kind or suitable environments were not available.

The season was yet young and both robins and doves needed to continue nesting. Mac and Huelota, another pair of doves, and a pair of robins found space in a farmyard five miles to the west of the destroyed grove. The robins built in a tamarisk tree, on a limb about six meters above the ground. It took several days of concerted effort on the part of both, for they spent much time collecting string and horsehair from around the barnyard, fiber from the trunk of a palm tree and mud from the watering trough for the livestock. The female molded these into a cup about her breast. While they were building Mac took a liking to the site. There wasn't much physical confrontation between the pairs until eggs had been laid: two blues of the robin and two whites of the dove. Both females trying to incubate ended in a wing slapping and pecking battle in which Huelota dominated, driving the robin away. She settled on the four eggs and pulled herself low behind the mud walls of the nest. The robin, unable to resist the hormonal urge to incubate, returned to brood on the limb close beside her nest. As darkness approached she left with her mate, seeking food and water, and did not return.

Having similar incubation periods, the first robin egg pipped two weeks later, but, unable to survive on pigeon milk, the tiny nestling starved by the end of the day. It was three days later before Mac's hatchling emerged and he had long since tossed out the dead robin. His brood fledged successfully early in June.

This multiple use of a nest site can work both ways. At a farmyard across the road a pair of doves built in a crotch of limbs high in a Chinese Elm and was successful in rearing two youngsters that flew in July. Later that month a pair of robins found the empty nest and used it as a foundation for their more impressive one. Their four, bright-eyed young left late in August and then the same or another pair of doves rented this vacant apartment. They assembled a few things in the bottom, laid an egg on September 4, and produced young that flew on the third day of October, long after California's dove season had opened. But these farmyards were protected places.

The other pair of doves at Mac's farmyard had a more bizarre experience. In a lemon tree they found a convenient limb at five meters that proved a good location and their first brood of two was fledged early in June. Four days later the pair was back and had incubated their eggs for ten days when a pair of House Sparrows thought that the same sloping limb had possibilities. They began their bulky straw house just above the doves' heads. The dovelets hatched and within the next week the ambitious sparrows had a structure that hung down to within six centimeters of the brooding bird's back. Putting up with this indignity, the doves continued their family activities and brought two more young off in July. The sparrows either finished their nesting efforts or gave up and departed their pile of hay which canopied the doves' third successful attempt, two more young flying in August. All of this activity went on in the farmyard where 19 young doves were known to fledge, with a loss of only three, and the cat population in the same farmyard numbered ten.

CHAPTER TWELVE
Zee and Ura

ZEE flew along the street toward his old nesting territory in Lewis. It had been twelve years since his mother and father had nested in an elm at the east end of town not far from a dilapidated old building that used to be the county seat. It had been a good year. Lewis was green with healthy trees and beautiful gardens, and Zee was one of three couplets of siblings that had been reared successfully in the same nest and sent on their way to see the world. He and his brother had flown on the second of September. Iowa was a state that protected its doves, and late-breeding pairs were not subject to the September holocausts like those in other states. It wasn't until migrating birds crossed state lines that they became acutely aware of the reality of guns and gunners. After a week of tutoring by his father, Zee went on his way south while his parents turned to a fifth brood, a healthy pair of sisters, hatched during the third week of the month. Zee never met his father again, nor did he know that as he flew on, his sisters and mother died on the nest beneath the claws of a marauding cat.

As he flew from tree to tree he remembered how things used to be and sensed how different his environment was. Now stately elms were mere shadows, either dead or partially covered with sickly leaves, victims of the dread Dutch-Elm disease, an Ascomycetes fungus carried on the bodies of tiny boring beetles that fed beneath the bark. Many had been cut down. Of 300, only a sick one remained in front of the local barber shop, planted by friends of the man who put rings on doves' legs. Only a few Silver Maples and Box-Elders appeared to be healthy and several of these had been topped by tree cutters to make them bushy, not realizing that such butchery opens the tree to invasion by numerous wood-boring insects and fungi that shorten its life.

Zee turned to the north to find his garden still green and attractive, its hackberries, pines, poplars, and maples planted long ago by someone who also loved trees. He was again without a mate and cooed loudly and urgently from singing posts used for many years. With so many trees gone the dove population had dwindled, but he still hoped to find an attractive widow. One morning in June a dove fed in the garden and he dropped to her side. She, Ura, was responsive to his ardent courting and neck rubbing. Within a day or so he turned to finding an appropriate nest location. He could hope to find new places only as the trees that had furnished him with so many nest sites through the years had been altered by wind or winter storms. One site in particular, on the outer part of a pine branch, had served him well in the past. He went to it again, not knowing that such was a widespread habit among doves. Of all the nest locations here in town, 14%

had been used in previous years. Ura was only about half
Zee's age, but she, too, had had many experiences during
her long migrations and several breeding seasons.

Zee called her to the familiar branch and they built
upon it. The pine was one of two that had been planted
close together. Only a few meters across from that of the
doves was a nest of Blue Jays, an enemy that had long
plagued Zee. It was hardly possible that the sharp-eyed
jays were unaware of Zee and Ura, even though they were
busy feeding their own nestlings, four of which flew on
July 25. Zee's two youngsters flew three days later.

To the human observer it would appear that there is
an infinite number of places in the fields and towns for
birds of many species to use as nesting sites. However,
much must be considered in the selection of such of a nest
location; its protection, the distance to food and water,
the preferences of the pair seeking a site, the exposure to
sun or wind, and many more. Multiple usage of preferred
sites by doves is evidence of their limited availibility. A
few may be so desirable as to be used year after year. In
Lewis, during one breeding season, 153 nests were placed
in the same locations as in the previous year, Following
are examples of this usage.

A homestead in a Colorado Blue Spruce at a seven
meter height on the east side of the tree came into use in
August by a pair that may have had earlier nesting fail-
ures. Two eggs (1) were present on the ninth, but one
had been stolen eleven days later and the second failed
to hatch. The following year this location was in use for
an extended period; two eggs (2) laid early in April were
chilled by a blizzard on 18 April even though both parents remained at the nest during the storm. On April 25,
the nest was again in use (3) and two young hatched, were
raised successfully and fledged on May 22. Almost immediately the birds were back with two eggs (4) on May 27

that were eaten by a squirrel two days later. Two eggs (5) were again in the nest on June 3 and four days later they were covered with mites *(Lipponysus sylviarum)* which the parents could have picked up while feeding in nearby chicken yards. Although some young are raised in the presence of these mites, this time some avian predator punctured the eggs five days later.

The nest site then went unused for over a month before two eggs (6) started the cycle anew in July. These hatched on August 4, but some predator took one on August 17 and the remaining nestling did not leave for another week. Two weeks later, its leg, bearing the numbered ring, was found under a tree; evidently it had met death soon after leaving the nest.

Early in April of its third year this site was again in use. Nest material had been added to the remnants that had survived the winter and eggs (7) were laid April 9-10, but the next day, parents and eggs were subjected to a freezing north wind. The following morning a Blue Jay was caught in the act of pecking at the incubating dove hovering over the eggs. The jay flew away, but later returned and took the eggs. The next attempt was seen May 11 (8) and the two eggs were punctured four days later. For the ninth time (9) in three years, on June 3, it was active. This time one young hatched and left normally on July 1. The tenth (10) use of the nest began in August and two young flew on the 31st. This location had been used ten times in three years but only three attempts were successful, raising five young.

The second location was three meters high in a Red Pine and the nest was under construction on 25 April. These eggs (1) hatched on May 10-11, but the nestlings lived only two days before some predator took them. On June 23, doves were trying again (2), and this time two young hatched on July 8. They grew rapidly and left ten days later. A few weeks after that, a pair of robins (3) built here and raised their family of four.

The second year the site was in use on April 15 with one dove egg (4). The robin nest had weathered the winter and, although broken down somewhat, still made a good location for the doves. A second egg was laid and a third on the 19th. When one young hatched two weeks later, the nest contained it and the two eggs. Six days later a fourth egg was laid and it was apparent that at least two females were using the nest. Whichever parent remained on duty, the young one thrived and flew on May 9, leaving four unhatched eggs.

The site was active again (5) early in June when three eggs were present. Apparently two pairs were still using the site, for eight days later there was a fourth egg. Probably competition over who was to incubate resulted in desertion. Maybe one pair won, for on August 8 there were two eggs (6) which hatched on the 25th. But the old robin nest, now piled high with accumulated dove building, was becoming weaker with each storm until it fell from the tree on the fourth of September. The young were uninjured by the fall and their parents brooded them on the ground. Two days later they were flying about, but one still was not destined to have a long life. It was shot near Calvert, Texas five weeks later (not two months old, and 700 miles south of its origin).

In the third year robins beat the doves to the site and built their mud and straw nest (7) in May. They raised five young but the doves may not have returned, because the site remained unclaimed for the rest of the year. It had produced five doves of 15 eggs and nine robins from nine eggs in seven tries.

*T*he thoughtlessness and cruelty of children is said to reflect the thoughtlessness and cruelty of their parents. This conclusion may be moot, but mankind's hand has never been kind toward other animals, especially those he fears, those he feeds upon, or those that he seeks for profit.

One summer, among the spreading limbs of a Box Elder near Zee's homeland, a neighboring pair of doves built at four meters and on May 14 the first egg was laid, but ten days later wind destroyed both eggs. The nest was rebuilt and another brood started three weeks later. Two nestlings hatched on July 4, and a third the following day. Of so similar an age, the three had a good chance of surviving. Three days later some passing boys threw clods of dirt at the nest, desisting only when they failed to knock it down. The next morning the birdman found that one clod had fallen into the nest, crushing one nestling. It was not yet dead, but was injured by the weight of the dirt and its nestmates crowded beside it. With the nest cleared of debris and the three replaced, they all seemed to thrive. On July 19 all were present and the following day two flew to safety. The third, the injured one, also attempted to leave with them but could not keep up, lagging behind until it fell and crawled beneath a lilac bush, there to die of exposure and hunger. The agony of wildlife subject to humans!

CHAPTER THIRTEEN
The
Dread Trichomonad

*T*ORTULA had met one of Ura's daughters in Mexico, but he had not become enamored of her and now he was going home. It was early February, his fourth trek north as he left central Mexico. His route, one of his longest flights made by doves in America; began near Mexico City and ended in a shelterbelt in northern North Dakota. He had been using this shelterbelt for three years and had left early in August each year to avoid gunners until he got to Oklahoma. As the shelterbelt had been a fruitful location with good nest sites, Tortula and his wife raised six young each season. This time his route was to take him north through Arizona, along the great Colorado River, into Wyoming, and northeast into North Dakota. It was a long, hazardous, and exciting journey, but he enjoyed the company of the doves he met along the way.

The flock thinned and most birds turned east or held north, but Tortula's bearings were west of north. The other birds crossed a little east of Big Bend, moving almost due north to their nesting grounds in cities, towns, farmyards, riparian forests, woodlands, even corn and wheat fields. Crossing into Arizona it was only a matter of a few hours flight to the city of Tucson. Tortula always enjoyed the stop here because there was an abundance of food and water. The Saguaro made interesting roosts and many of his acquaintances stopped here to establish their territories and nest in hollows provided by the giant cacti.

This was a land of many doves. He could drop to a vacant lot or field covered with stiff desert shrubs and, walking beneath their sparse shade, feed with the somewhat larger White-winged Doves, which often resented him and joined in active wing-slapping. There were two tiny doves that reminded him of his own young when about to fledge; the Common Ground Dove with rich chestnut underwings that were revealed in flight, and the little Barred Ground Dove sometimes called a Zebra Dove because of its meticulous barring over the body and back.

As he dropped into the city, he became aware that he was seeing very few of the other kinds of doves. A sweeping wing whistling brake dropped him among the shrubs of one of his favorite feeding places. A House Sparrow fluttered away and a Mockingbird caroled from a power pole, but no doves moved. Nearby was a Ground Dove, dead on its side. Tortula walked up to it to see that it was but a dry husk. Beyond, nearly hidden by a dry stem, was a White-winged Dove. It too, was dead. Looking around he could see that near a sidewalk was a Barred Dove also shriveled in death. Death he recognized but could not understand. What was happening here?

Discouraged, he flew to another vacant lot and found the same situation; dead doves of all species, including Mourning Doves. He saw nothing that he could fear and touched the bodies or fed among them. Watering places included bird baths and curbside puddles.

Tortula could not know that he had entered an area suffering from an epizootic (epidemic) of *Trichomonas columbae*. This is a microscopic organism, a protistan with a long, undulating fin, a flagellum, with which it swims or propels itself through water. This species is a parasite of doves, hence its name, *columbae,* of doves. The rest of its name, *tricho,* hair or filament, *monas,* single or one; i.e., the "single-haired parasite of doves." Unfortunately, once it has invaded a dove (its host), it produces numerous eggs or cysts and the resulting organisms feed among the pigeon-milk producing tissues, gradually destroying them. The crop and throat fill with a cheese-like residue that clogs them. Unable to feed or drink, the poor dove slowly starves. When the infected birds try to drink from bird baths or puddles the trichomonads swim out into the water and the place then becomes infectious. When uninfected birds try to drink there, they suck up the trichomonads and are infected themselves. If a bird is healthy and thrifty it may resist these parasites and live with a few of them. Sometimes the parasites become stronger and can attack healthy birds. This is what was happening at Tucson.

Tortula fed among the victims and drank from the pools and he found that many doves of all four species about the city and surrounding desert had thinned in ranks. He remained only a few days and moved north with other travelers. They skirted the Grand Canyon, stopped for water and food along the Colorado River, passing the amazing arches of red sandstone and continued out onto the rolling semi-desert and grasslands of Wyoming. Several of his companions fell ill and dropped behind, while others turned off toward their breeding grounds. Finally, the vast plains of North and South Dakota rolled beneath them and shelterbelts stretched for miles. Tortula arrived at the one he knew on the fifth of April, and set to work repairing his boundaries. It was another month before winter really let go of this land and he waited impatiently for his mate of last year. She failed to return so he sought another. His new mate was the same age as he and they raised their first brood of the year in a Russian Olive. The second clutch, in a small spruce, was just hatching when their mother began to feel ill.

All those months ago, Tortula had drunk the water from the puddles in Tucson, puddles infected with the trichomonads from the dying Barred Doves. These parasites had established themselves in the walls of his crop, but he was healthy and his body had isolated and confined them. They continued to grow and survive at a low level, however. During his billing and courtship feeding of his new mate, he had unknowingly infected her with his parasites. They, in turn, infected their first brood of youngsters, which was able to throw off the parasites and they left the nest as healthy fledglings. Day after day, their mother had grown worse as she incubated the new clutch of eggs. At hatching she appeared disoriented and hardly helped the chicks. Tortula performed his daily duties, but his mate did not do well at night. She could not swallow seeds and drank with difficulty. Her crop was filling with detritus, which she could neither cough up or pass on. Unable to survive on food from only Tortula, both babies died during their third night. Their mother remained on them until Tortula came to brood. He discovered their inactivity and left. She had dropped to the ground and tried to feed. She could pick up seeds, but not swallow them.

Other doves, recognizing that she was ill, slapped at her and drove her away, their only prophylaxis to prevent the spread of something they did not understand. Driven beneath a multiflora rose, she was slowly starving, and was mercifully relieved of her suffering when a fox found her.

As the flock that Tortula had been with that spring entered the great plains of eastern Wyoming, some members "peeled off" to fly toward their home territories. Some of his friends turned east into Nebraska before they reached the vast plains of the Dakotas. Those headed toward the Platte River and farther south found territories in woodlands and shaded towns, but north of the Platte stretches of farmlands give way to the ocean of rolling, almost-treeless sandhills. Here road bridges came into use as nest sites. These bridges spanned creeks and were built of heavy wooden beams, the upper surfaces of which were sought out by Eastern and Say's Phoebes, robins, House Wrens, as well as House Sparrows and the doves. At one such bridge the doves fledged young on August 3 and September 7, and at another on August 1 and September 1. Where they had nested before these late dates is uncertain. A third bridge of steel and concrete was less desirable and there two pairs tried to occupy one site and deserted the nest of four eggs because they couldn't agree on incubation.

The following year the same pairs continued to use the under supports of these bridges. From the supports of one bridge, two broods were raised and flew on June 2 and July 2. Two pairs preferred another bridge nearby, one fledging one young on June 18 and the other sending off their youngsters two days later. The first pair returned to use their place again, successfully fledging young on July 12 and September 4. Under the steel bridge the resident pair nested two times, two broods flying on July 10 and August 24.

CHAPTER FOURTEEN

The Grackles

IT was spring again, early in fact, for it had snowed in Lewis only a few days before. Last year's nests of any species that had stood the ravages of winter were much in demand. In the top of a tall apple behind the church were the remnants of a Bronzed Grackle nest, the mud-packed foundation of which was still intact. One of Zee's traveling friends had arrived early and he and his mate found this to their liking. They began adding a few sticks to it, but without much enthusiasm. In May two grackles took over. They could have been the rightful owners from the previous year, but the doves contested this. After some wing-slapping the doves retreated and the female grackle set about building a new nest on the foundation of the old. This took her several days followed by five days of laying five spotted, bluish eggs and two weeks of incubation. The shiny black male followed his hard-working mate when she was off duty, but did not participate in her activities. However, he did help her occasionally while the juveniles were learning to be self sufficient.

All of this transpired while the doves had found another location in the orchard and raised their two young. The male returned to inspect the recently-vacated grackle nest (now in much better condition than when he had attempted to use it earlier), but the grackles were not as clean as he would have desired. He and his mate began renovating the quarters on June 10. Again, they fledged two youngsters by July 4, and immediately prepared the nest for their third brood. This enterprise lasted through the heat of summer and of their eggs only one hatched. Receiving care from both parents, it tried its wings on August 10. The pair, with their latest young, took a holiday and flew to the surrounding farmlands, where the flowers of spring were ripening the seeds of late summer.

Returning to town, they found the apartment already occupied by another pair of doves. This late in the summer only doves continue to raise families and these new tenants had two eggs on September 9, again only one of which hatched. Its nest life was uneventful, for squirrels and jays were busy harvesting other foods, allowing this little male to fledge on October 3. After such heavy use all summer, the venerable old nest failed to weather the next winter. Spring found both doves and grackles examining the remains.

CHAPTER FIFTEEN

The Story Closes

ZEE lived a long and fruitful life and survived several wives. One was very tragically struck by an automobile and flung to the curbside where he found her. He cooed to her, tried to preen her and even feed her, but to no avail. So he sat in solitary grief beside her stiffening body until a passing dog frightened him away.

In the main, Zee's life was happy, busy, and full of many experiences and hazards, with all of which he managed to cope. For nearly 20 million years (since the lower

Miocene), his ancestors had lived on this land, building nests in the forest edges. They even nested on limbs torn from the trees by giant animals of those times, animals that became extinct while his clan held on. His ancestors had seen the rise of the two-legged creature that now dominated the landscape and so altered the face of the earth.

Zee was tired; his years were weighing heavily upon him. Sixteen times he had made the round trip into Mexico. This was his seventeenth: 50,000 miles of travel in a lifetime. He had joined a group of younger birds somewhere in Texas and they brought him farther south and east than had been his usual route. They were crossing a low range of wooded hills in Tlaxcala into the Potrero Hondo valley with the magnificent snow-capped Citlaltépetl Volcano looming in the background. They were far east of the valley in Jalisco that had been his haven all of these winters, one that his son Ha-Wo had used so long ago and Naida, too. The flock paused to rest in the dead crown of an old oak. Zee gazed up at the great mountain which was new to him. It was September 15 and he had left Iowa in August when he and his mate had fledged a pair of healthy youngsters and gone to the fields to rest. But, as he fed among the wheat stubble, something drove him to join the migrants from the north that called to him. It had been a long, hard trip from Iowa this year with many storms and heavy winds. He dozed, letting the younger birds warn if danger approached.

Nestor, a poor farmer of the valley stepped up to his patient red mare, saddled her, and swung into the saddle carrying a single-shot, 10-gauge shot gun in his right hand. They had had little meat of late, for his meager oat crop did not allow many luxuries. Maybe today he could hunt successfully. A mile or so from his adobe hut Nestor noticed that several doves had flown into a tree by the edge of the woods. Riding closer he took careful aim and, as he pulled the trigger, wondered why they had not flushed as he approached. Zee, sensing danger, looked back and started to fly just as the pellets struck him. Two others fell as well. Nestor got off the horse to pick up the three birds and put them into a bag that he carried. Riding on he found no other game and returned home, handing his wife the bag and commenting that they weren't much, but three doves would help flavor their evening meal. She turned to clean them and soon called him from the yard.

"Look, Nestor! One is wearing a silver bracelet on its leg!" They both examined the ring and he removed it, saying that it had numbers written on it and might be something important. Not knowing what to do about it he dropped it into a drawer in the cabinet by the stove.

Months later, the circuit-riding priest of the parish, an old friend of Nestor and his family, came by and stopped for supper and an evening of talk. They were discussing the scarcity of wild game when Nestor remembered the silver ring found the previous fall. Searching through the drawer he located it and showed it to the cleric. Brother Timothy was well read and recognized it as a message from America, saying he would send it there and let Nestor know what came of it. So Zee came back into the world of knowledge even though it saddened the man who banded birds to learn that a dove he knew in his youth was no more. Zee had been banded when six days old, on August 20, 17 years before.

Postscript

GRIEVE not for Zee, but grieve for the 40 million Mourning Doves that are shot every year by men, women, and teenagers who rate this act as a pleasurable sport or pastime!

Because it is considered a gamebird by many and because it is a migratory species, the Mourning Dove comes under the "management" of the United States Fish and Wildlife Service This "management" has never been more than survey and regulation of hunting seasons. In the spring months the personnel of the Fish and Wildlife Service (FWS), in cooperation with field workers, count the number of singing males along established rural routes in almost every state. From these data, and the results of nesting studies to calculate production and breeding success, bag limits and the length of the hunting season for the nation are established. Each State Game Commission or its equivalent can open a dove hunting season within the limits of the national regulations.

Mourning Doves are hunted in all continuous states except Minnesota, Iowa, Wisconsin, Michigan, Ohio, and the eight northeastern states. The National Regulation sets the season at 70 days anytime from September 1 to the 15th of January, and permits states to divide the 70 days into three seasons within that time span. Bag limits are usually around 10 birds a day. The way hunting is permitted varies among the states as the game regulators review and interpret the national rules.

Because of this flexibility in regulations that permit a state to open three short seasons totaling 70 days or one long season at any time between 1 September and 15 January, the bird is under fire almost continuously during migration and wintering for the whole five months. These same game managers proudly point out that over three million people (about one percent of the nation's population) enjoys 19 million days of dove shooting and are privileged to "harvest" ten percent of the nation's doves (more than 40 million birds, not counting those that die later of injuries received from scatter guns).

The Mourning Dove is an ancient species and has adjusted to its life on the open parklands and forest edge. Its nests were built mainly among the low trees bordering forests or woodlands. For thousands, even millions of years it has been doing this. Mourning Dove bones have been found in the Rancho La Brea tar pits and among Pleistocene deposits in caves in Arizona. During these past epochs they have been contemporaries of the saber-toothed tiger, the giant cave bear, glyptodonts, megatheria, mammoths, and the savage dire wolf, all of which have since become extinct. When glaciers covered and scoured much of North America, the doves moved into southern lands only to push north again as the ice receded. From their nests in wooded glades they could look out over prairies inhabited with great herds of bison, primitive horses, camels, mammoths, and other grazers. The next time that a Mourning Dove coos from a tree in your yard, pause to remember that his ancestors were cooing from similar trees a thousand times as long ago as the first recorded history of man.

Through these long millenia doves have learned to cope with weather, predators, and parasites by developing a long breeding season, a wide geographical tolerance, a rapid childhood, a specialized method of feeding young superimposed on a diet of easily-obtained seeds, and the ability to migrate to more favorable climates or environments. In spite of its great geological age this bird has retained genetic malleability.

Before Eurpoeans overwhelmed the North American continent, the dove's close relative, the Passenger Pigeon, had reached numbers never before seen among birds through a specialized way of life. It is estimated that Passenger Pigeons numbered in the billions, but to do so they were under great restrictive requirements. They laid only one egg, bred only in great flocks, were unable to live in small groups, and migrated through the great deciduous forests of eastern North America, following the production of acorns, beech, and other nuts. When man moved en massse west during the second half of the last century, the Passenger Pigeon staggered before his massive exploitation and environmental destruction and became extinct. In lesser abundance both east and west, its smaller cousin the Mourning Dove not only followed man, but seemed to have adopted him. Instead of immense blocks of solid forests, mankind left smaller clumps. This was to the doves' liking. Europeans entered the prairie and, not satisfied with it, tore up its sods, farmed, planted trees, and brought in new food plants and attendant seeds. Again this was to the doves' advantage. When drought or continued lumbering reduced these habitats, the doves moved to towns and farmyards where trees were watered an nurtured. All of which resulted in a vastly extended forest edge in the eyes of the doves.

During environmental alterations, the game manager has made no intensive or extensive effort to find ways of improving the doves' living conditions, should these changes exceed the birds' tolerance. He has only tried to control the gun. The Mourning Dove population seemed to stand up before all of this abuse and change. Said another way, before Zee and all of the others met their fates before the gun, cat, car, or other accidents, they managed to raise enough families to replace these losses and themselves. In spite of this, environmental pressures are so great that dove populations are slowly diminishing over vast areas of North America. In the recent understatement of officialdom, FWS experts admit, "Causes of decline in dove abundance cannot be isolated with certainty. Likely, a combination of factors involving both mortality and reproduction is responsible."

It has been the fate of all species of doves the world over to have mankind intervene in their ecosystems and to find their flesh palatable. One by one, species by species, they have faltered before this assault and many have faded away entirely.

All wild creatures are subject to the hazards of out-of-door living, including the unseen attacks of diseases and parasites, but it is only in the past few thousand years that they have had to cope with so violent and persistent a predator as man. Man *(Homo sapiens),* because of his protective shields (houses, traffic lights, laws, efficient medicine and surgery, methods of abundant food production and distribution) has habitually overlooked the excessive hazards that he creates for wildlife. Conservation is an effort to reduce the adverse effects of humans upon other creatures of this earth and to enhance wild living.

Our successful, hot-blooded descendents of little dinosaurs that we call birds, are highly organized with superhuman abilities of sight, hearing, and reaction. By extrapolation from these abilities we may assume that their memories, awareness, and powers of decision-making are also acute. These abilities are evident in the actions of pet birds or wild birds tolerant of human observation. It is only necessary to watch a normal pet bird (not pinioned, caged, or doped) make selections and decisions during its daily life. To project these same capabilities to wild birds of similar or same species is valid. Birds are bound by the restrictions of genetic control, as Mac's inability to care for young when Huelota was gone. We had one female Mourning Dove which would care for any young without relationship to diurnal rhythms or nestling age, but males could not make this hurdle. Both sexes can cooperate in decisions concerning nest location and both can recall where they nested the season before.

Unless color-marked, and then for only a short time, information about a bird after it has left the nest comes either as the marked bird is recaptured at its home or from band recoveries. Recovery records are almost always available only after the bird is dead. Most people who find a banded bird alive or dead neglect to report the ring's number an location to the Fish and Wildlife Service, Washington, DC, thereby reducing the information from these recoveries to less than one percent of the birds banded. Recovered doves range in age from less than a year to as old as 20 years. Captive individuals have lived beyond this. Most of the records received from the thousands of birds that I have banded indicate that they have lived about five years. Once we have this information forwarded from the Bird Banding Office in Patuxent, the birds are no longer part of the picture, for they are dead. How much longer they might have lived is suggested by Zee's age. Almost all records from birds that I banded reveal that they were shot in September or October at some geographical point other than their nesting home. Can we assume that these birds had established breeding territories near where they were recovered? I have made this assumption in some instances, but they could have been migrants many miles from their breeding homes.

I wish to acknowledge the assistance of and thank the following friends and associates for their kindness in taking time from their busy schedules to review the *Whistling Wings* manuscript and to make constructive comments about it: Richard Setlowe, author of *The Experiment* and *The Haunting of Susan Blackwell;* Hope Ryden, author of *God's Dog, Mustangs - America's Last Wild Horses,* and other books on wildlife; Dr. Glen C. Sanderson, wildlife biologist; Marian Weston, conservation activist; Kathleen Clement, artist; Dr. Ralph Buchsbaum, editor and scientist; Karen Morgan, artist; and I.B. Sinclair for financial assistance from the Committee for Dove Protection.

Appendix

*T*HE scientific name of the Mourning Dove is *Zenaida macroura* (Linne). I am often asked, "Just how do animals get these unprounceable scientific names?" It is a long, but interesting story extending over three centuries. Early in the 18th century several biologists were busy cataloging the known animals and plants and trying to bring order out of a chaos of names, but each biolgist was using a different system. The classification of living things set up by Aristotle 1,200 years before was still in use, but world exploration and the discovery of many new species made this system awkward and inadequate.

Among these catalogers was a Swede by the name of Carl von Linne, or Carlus Linnaeus as his name is Latinized. He was doing more than just naming animals and plants, he was attempting to describe them as well. During this century Latin was still a universal language for most scientists and learned men. Greek was used less often, but was understood by most. Linnaeus wrote his animal and plant descriptions in Latin, often using Greek terms. He published these descriptions in a series of volumes entitled *Systema Naturae* and by 1756 he had published nine editions. Each was different in the treatment of species names because he could not settle on a definite system of naming them. Finally, in 1757, he published his tenth edition and in this he established a system in which every animal or plant had a name made up of the first two words of his description. In writing about the animal or plant it was referred to by these two words. Hence, the dog became *Canis familiaris* and the cat *Felis domesti-*

cus. Later the first name became known as the genus and the second word as the species and the system was called binomial nomenclature. Because of this easy consistent method, all biologists began to recognize the tenth edition of Linnaeus' *Systema Naturae* as authoritative and today all animal or plant names have no earlier author than Linnaeus. The value of this system springs from the fact that animals and plants have colloquial names known only to the people who use that dialect, while every biologist will recognize the scientific name no matter what his nationality. Since 1757 a host of modifications have been built up around Linnaeus' method. The diversity of living things has also required modification in thought and method, based on the way scientists interpret the system. Today, to be correctly written a name should be italicized and have the genus capitalized. The species name follows the genus and should agree with it in number and gender. The two italicized names are then followed by the name of the person who described the animal or plant. If someone reviewed the species and decided it is in the wrong genus, the genus name may be changed, and the original author's name is put in parenthesis.

This brings us back to how and when the Mourning Dove got its name *Zenaida macroura* (Linne). Linneaus originally described the bird, but he put it in a different genus, from which it was later removed. Linnaeus could not possibly have seen all of the animals of the world known at his time, or even mounted specimens, so he described and named new ones, many from North America, based on drawings brought back to Europe by naturalists and explorers. In his twelfth edition of *Systema Natura,* published in 1766, he described a dove from a picture drawn by naturalist Mark Catesby (1683-1749), who extensively explored North America. Catesby had made the drawing in the Carolinas, so Linnaeus called the bird

Columba carolinensis or Carolina Dove. Later it was discovered that in his tenth edition Linnaeus had described a dove of the West Indies from a painting by the man by the name of Edwards and this bird he called *Columba macroura*, referring to the long tail (Greek: *makros,* large; *urus,* tail). The two descriptions were of the same species, therefore the earlier one, *Columba macroura,* became the accepted name.

How *Zenaida* came about is a lovely story. Napoleon Bonaparte had a brother, Lucien, whose first son was Charles Lucien Bonaparte (1803-1857). When a teenager he was sent to Italy to study the sciences, including natural history. Another of Napoleon's brothers was King Joseph of Spain whose eldest daughter, Zenaida, fell in love with and married the handsome Charles, then 19. They sailed to America where he became a famous ornithologist and wrote about both American and European birds. On the Caribbean Islands he found a beautiful dove which he named *Zenaida aurita* after his lovely wife, a memorial that has lasted 150 years and will last as long as people love and protect birds. The Zenaida Dove looks much like a Mourning Dove, only more colorful, with a white, trailing edge to the wings. In 1854 Bonaparte reviewed the American doves and decided that they were not *Columba*. He created the genus *Zenaidura* and put the Mourning Dove in it, accepting the twelfth edition Linnean name *carolinensis* and the bird became *Zenaidura carolinensis* (Linne).

Later Robert Ridgeway (1850-1929) of the Smithsonian Museum discovered this error and in 1885 he published the name *Zenaidura macroura* (Linne) which remained the official name for many years. Upon examining specimens of Mourning Dove-like birds in the museum, other biologists decided that the Mourning Dove and the White-winged Dove *(Zenaida asiatica)* were so similar to the Zenaida Dove that they should be grouped together. From Central America through much of South America is another dove resembling the Mourning Dove, leading ornithologists to believe that the two may be a super-species of the same origin. A small cluster of very similar doves is now recognized: Zenaida Dove *(Zenaida aurita)* of the Caribbean Islands; Eared Dove *(Z. auriculata)* of South America; White-winged Dove *(Z. asiatica)* of Mexico; Mourning Dove *(Z. macroura)* of North America; and isolated and endangered species on the Galapagos Islands *(Z. galapogoensis)*; and some think that the extinct Passenger Pigeon *(Ectopistes migratorius)* may also have been a large species of this group.

SUGGESTED FURTHER READING

*T*HERE is an extensive scientific literature concerning the Mourning Dove and annually the sporting or hunting magazines feature articles about it. Following are publications that the reader might find interesting.

Bent, Arthur C. Life histories of North American gallinaceus birds (orders Galliformes and Collumbiformes). *US National Museum Bulletin,* **162**: 402-416, 1932.

Blockstein, David. Gone forever, a contemporary look at the extinction of the Passenger Pigeon. *American Birds,* **39**: 845-851, 1985.

Dalyrymple, Byron W. *Doves and Dove Shooting.* G.P. Putnam's Sons, New York, 1949.

Delacour, Jean. *Wild Pigeons and Doves.* All-Pet Books, Inc., Fond du Lac, WI, 1959.

Fish and Wildlife Service. Mourning Dove breeding population status. *Annual Administrative Reports,* 1963 through 1990.

Goodwin, Derek. *Pigeons and Doves of the World,* British Museum of Natural History Publication, **663,** 1967.

Marte, Judith H., John D. Newsom, and Phillip J. Zwank. Late season Mourning Dove nesting in southern Louisiana. *Wildlife Society Bulletin,* **13** (1): 58-62, 1985.

McClure, H. Elliott. Cooing activity and censusing of the Mourning Dove. *Journal of Wildlife Management,* **3**: 323-328, 1939.

McClure, H. Elliott. Mourning Dove production in south-western Iowa. *Auk,* **59**: 64-75, 1942.

McClure, H. Elliott. Ecology and management of the Mourning Dove in Cass County, Iowa. *Iowa State University Research Bulletin,* **310**, 1943.

McClure, H. Elliott. The effect of tree removal on a Mourning Dove population. *Auk,* **61**: 561-564, 1944.

McClure, H. Elliott. Mourning Doves in Nebraska and the West. *Auk,* **63**: 24-42, 1946.

McClure, H. Elliott. An eleven-year summary of Mourning Dove observations in the West. *Transactions of the 15th North American Wildlife Conference,* 335-346, 1950.

Mirarchi, R.E. and P.F. Scanlon. Duration of Mourning Dove crop gland activity during nesting cycle. *Journal of Wildlife Management,* **44**: 209-213, 1980.

Westmoreland, David, Louis B. Best, and David E. Blockstein. Multiple breeding as a reproductive strategy: Time conserving adaptations in Mourning Doves. *Auk,* **103**: 196-203, 1980.

Williams, Ted. The quick metamorphosis of Indiana's doves. *Audubon,* **87**: 38-45, 1985.